Science and Wisdom

Science and Wisdom

Jürgen Moltmann

Translated by
Margaret Kohl

scm press

Translated by Margaret Kohl
From the German *Wissenschaft und Weisheit*
Published by Christian Kaiser/Gütersloher Verlagshaus GmbH,
Gütersloh 2002

Translation © Margaret Kohl 2003

British Library Cataloguing in Publication data

A catalogue record for this book is available
from the British Library

0 334 02918 X

First British edition published 2003
by SCM Press
9–17 St Albans Place, London N1 0NX

www.scm-canterburypress.co.uk

SCM Press is a division of
SCM-Canterbury Press Ltd

Printed and bound in Great Britain by
Biddles Ltd, www.biddles.co.uk

This book is dedicated to the University of Nottingham in gratitude for the conferral of the honorary degree of Doctor of Divinity and in remembrance of my beginnings in the theological school behind barbed wire in Norton Camp, 1946–1948.

Contents

THE WISDOM OF THE SCIENCES

Preface

From very early on, the theological discussion with scientists fascinated me. When I was a schoolboy I dreamed of studying mathematics and physics. When I was called up in 1943, at the age of 16, I was just reading Louis de Broglie's book *Matière et Lumière*, which had recently appeared in German with a foreword by Werner Heisenberg. But then experiences of life and death in war and captivity overwhelmed me. Existential questions became more important than scientific ones, and these existential questions led me to theology. But for all that, the scientific questions were never forgotten. Unfortunately I never found the time to study physics thoroughly, either parallel to theology or afterwards. So in this respect I remained a dilettante, and am still so today – an amateur in the double sense of the word: though lacking professional expertise in the scientific field, science is nevertheless for me a subject of interest and delight. Later, I took every opportunity of entering as theologian into dialogue with scientists, read standard scientific books with interest, and tried to understand them. All this convinced me that theologians can learn something about God not just from the Bible but from 'the book of nature' too.

For a long time, in the wake of Karl Barth's famous – or notorious – 'no' to natural theology in 1934, any expectations of this kind were deeply suspect in German Protestant theology. It was the discovery of the ecological crisis of the environment, among living things other than ourselves and in nature as a whole, which for the first time provoked a new theology of nature, and called to life a new creation spirituality. It sounds

somewhat presumptuous, and smacks of unasked-for inter-
ference, if in the light of this crisis theologians try to confront the
scientists with a 'natural theology'. But what I have in mind is
not so much a special theology; it is rather a general teaching of
wisdom. And for that reason I have deliberately called this book
'Science and Wisdom'.

The essays collected here were written over a long period of
time, and are no more than contributions to the important but
still highly insecure dialogue between theologians and scientists.
In these discussions I have not attempted to find a religious
interpretation for scientific findings, but have tried to relate
theological insights to these findings, so as to make theology
compatible with the sciences. Listening to scientists, I have tried
to present the profile of theology which is turned towards them.
So my concern was always to reformulate theology in a scientific
respect.

Important for me was the FEST (Forschungsstätte der
Evangelischen Studiengemeinschaft) in Heidelberg, where in the
1970s the inter-faculty *Theory of Open Systems* (1974) was
developed. I owe a great deal to Georg Picht, Carl-Friedrich von
Weizsäcker, Günter Howe and Klaus A. M. Müller. The 1990s
saw another assembly point, at the Center of Theological Inquiry
in Princeton, under its director Wallace Alston, with the group
round John Polkinghorne and William Stoeger, and with
American and German theologians. Through my participation in
the project 'The End of the World and the Ends of God. Science
and Theology on Eschatology' (published in 2000) I attended a
number of conferences held under the auspices of the John
Templeton Foundation, and through these meetings was able to
participate in the dialogues taking place in the British and
American world – dialogues which differ considerably from their
German counterparts.

It was through the mediation of Ernst Wolf and Helmut
Gollwitzer, however, that earlier I became involved in the
medical-theological dialogue, and during the 1970s and 1980s
took part in a number of medical congresses in Davos, Zurich,
Basle and Montecatini. These contacts then also drew me into

the field of Christian diaconal service and took me to conferences held by associations for the disabled in Germany (see my book *Diakonie im Horizont des Reiches Gottes*, 1984).

In all these different fields I have tried to perceive the existential questions, to take up the implicit theological concerns, and to find theological approaches for the necessary dialogue. I am therefore publishing these papers, asking forbearance for all that I have left unsaid and undeveloped, and hoping that these contributions may encourage others to set out for themselves, and to follow their own paths into what we must surely call this new theological territory.

Jürgen Moltmann
Tübingen, 1 July 2001

I

Theology in the World of the Modern Sciences[1]

1. Two Different Ways

The scientific explanation of the forces of nature and the constitution of the human being, of social conditions and historical movements – all that is the fate of modern times. Scientific and technological civilization is the task facing it. What meaning can Christian theology have in a world which has become the world of human beings, and will become so more and more? Where is the compulsion for theological reflection in a world where people no longer have to live with gods and demons, or with mysterious forces in nature and human destiny, but where we are living with 'the bomb' and with revolution? A world in which human beings are no longer dependent on nature, but where nature is dependent on human beings, and where human beings are increasingly delivered over to themselves and to what people like themselves do?

If we hear a topic like 'theology and science' mentioned, or 'faith and reason', what immediately springs to mind is the long history of conflict between the declining religious culture of the middle ages and the rising, autonomous scientific culture of modern times. We think of the trial of Galileo, and of modern slogans such as 'knowledge is power', or 'faith and science are irreconcilable'. We remind ourselves that the significance of theology in the modern scientific world is really its increasing insignificance for that world. The time is past when people disputed as to whether Copernicus was right, or the Book of Joshua when it tells in its tenth chapter that the sun and the moon stood still until the people had revenged themselves on their enemies. Today the dilemma between theology and science is no longer that they present conflicting statements. It is rather the lack of conflict between statements which stand side by side without any relation to one another, and which no longer have anything to say to each other at all. Faith and knowledge of the world are no longer locked in a conflict about the truth. They are resting side by side in a vacant co-existence.

How did the initial conflict turn into this frigid schism between the assurance of salvation and responsibility for the world, belief and thinking, theology and science?

According to Kant, the 'revolution in our way of thinking' was ushered in by Copernicus's book *De revolutionibus orbium coelestium*, which was published in 1543 by the Nuremberg Reformer Andreas Osiander. In his foreword (which Copernicus himself repudiated), the theologian expounded the meaning of the new world picture by way of the rhetorical concept of the hypothesis: hypotheses are the basis for calculations (*fundamenta calculi*), not articles of faith (*articuli fidei*). Faith does not tie the sciences down to a particular world-view which faith finds necessary; it sets the sciences free to arrive at knowledge of the world against the open horizons of hypothetical working drafts. Faith frees the sciences from the burden of dogmatically promulgated world-views, and constitutes its mobility in its progression from hypothesis to hypothesis.[2] But if faith is no longer the *magistra* which defines the foundations and purposes of scientific endeavour – if it now merely guarantees science its undisputed liberty – from what does faith itself take its bearings?

Johannes Kepler already perceived that God's intention with the Bible could not have been to correct erroneous opinions which were subject to their time, and thus to spare human beings the need for scientific investigation. His purpose could only be to reveal to men and women what was necessary for their eternal salvation.[3] The content of the Bible was therefore reduced to the question about human salvation – and the Bible's authority was simultaneously excluded from every sphere which does not have to do with salvation in the personal, supernatural realm. At the time this reduction was felt to be a great relief; and this is still the case today. It was viewed as the only possible way of maintaining the validity of the Bible at all. But with this reduction theology cut itself loose from the task of penetrating and mastering the world through insight into it. Theology's domain became a personal, supernatural doctrine of salvation. It could interpret salvation only as the salvation of the soul. And just because of this, science and the shaping of the world ceased to find any place in the framework of hope for the possible salvation of the universe and fear of possible doom. The less this salvation was thought of as having any reference to the world, the more knowledge of the world and the way the world was shaped became a matter of indifference as irrelevant for salvation. In addition, since Christian expectation of salvation depends on a historical remembrance defined by the name of Jesus Christ, theology and the sciences now got caught up in the conflict between tradition and personal experience. As long as minds were formed by texts, tradition reigned supreme. When, instead of texts, the formative influence increasingly became experience and experiment, people were liberated from tradition.[4] When Galileo wanted to show his opponents the Jupiter satellites, they refused to look through the telescope because they believed, as Bertolt Brecht put it, 'that there was no truth to be found in nature but only in the comparison of texts'.[5]

Blaise Pascal then gave this divide its classic definition: 'If we see this distinction clearly, we shall lament the blindness of those who in physics would allow only the truth of tradition instead of reason and experiment; and we shall be appalled at the folly of those who in theology put the arguments of reason in place of Scriptural tradition and the Fathers.'[6] It is only through the question about personal salvation that the human being finds access to religion, for in all perceptible reality God is not manifest 'as the Deists and the Jews say'; he is profoundly hidden.[7] For Descartes too, the religious question was the question about God and the human soul.[8] We can only speak of an assurance of God in a context of radical doubt and the human subject's certainty of itself. To wrestle with the question of the true Deity and the salvation of the whole in knowledge of the world's reality becomes senseless once this world is abstracted into the objective world of the *res extensae* and made merely the object of the *res cogitans*. The cleft between subject and object, *res cogitans* and *res extensa*, the humanities and the sciences, was the reason for the inward and outward disorganization of the modern world; for this materialism where nature is concerned abstracts from the history of the whole and, as Marx said, is 'hostile to human beings'.[9] 'The non-spiritual view of nature which Descartes in particular brought into vogue was bound to have as consequence a view of the mind and spirit without nature, and a view of mind, spirit *and* nature without God.'[10]

In modern times theology has gone along with this dichotomy in the awareness of the modern mind. It surrendered the knowledge that truth is always *one* and has to be the truth of *the whole*. It surrendered the expectation of a whole salvation or the salvation of the whole. The different spheres of truth developed in amicable divorce: Pascal's esprit du coeur – esprit de géometrie; Leibniz's vérités de fait – vérités de raison; Lessing's fortuitous truths of history – necessary truths of reason; Kant's practical reason – theoretical reason; mysticism and mathematics; existence and the scientific knowledge of existence; subjectivity and reification; positivism and decisionism.

Schleiermacher praised this double track in the modern mind: 'If the Reformation . . . does not have as its purpose the establishment of an eternal contract between the living Christian faith and scientific study, freed on every side, working on its own in complete independence, so that the former does not hinder the latter, and the latter does not exclude the former, then it is failing to meet the needs of our time, and we require yet another reformation, however it may develop and out of whatever struggles.'[11] Contemporary theology has hardly moved beyond this position. Rudolf Bultmann tells us: 'There is no protest against the secular sciences from the side of Christianity, because the eschatological interpretation of the world is not a way of explaining it, and because detachment from the world cannot be brought about through an interpretation of the world but only in the decision of the moment.'[12] And in Karl Barth we read: 'There is free scope for natural science beyond what theology has to describe as the work of the Creator. And theology can and must move freely where a science which really is science, and not secretly a pagan Gnosis or religion, has its appointed limits.'[13]

But, talking about a view of this kind, Carl Friedrich von Weizsäcker had already commented: 'A cleft between existence and nature which would make existence the field of the Christian faith and nature the field of the exact sciences assigns to both faith and science a field that is too narrow, and one which does not in fact exist at all in this form.'[14] Scientifically there can be no clean cut between objectivity and subjectivity, for the object of science is, after all, not nature as such but nature as it is exposed to human questioning. This means, as Heisenberg said, that here too the human being again encounters himself. Theologically, the separation is won at the cost of a self-mutilation, for it is hardly possible to offer to a world which knows nothing of salvation, salvation without a world, or to present to a godless reality an unreal God. If God and salvation cannot be interpreted in their reference to the whole, torn apart and open as it is here, then they cannot be interpreted at all. A retreat into the inwardness of the human heart leads faith into a ghetto in which it spoils and decays.

Philosophically, finally, we can assent to Hegel in his insight into the dialectic of the Enlightenment, when he maintains that we cannot escape this dichotomy by throwing in our lot with the one side or the other, in order that the other side, whichever it may be, can be silenced as unessential or dispensable; on the contrary, subjectivity and objectivity, spontaneity and rationality are historically dependent on each other and, in their mutual conditioning, together make up the whole of historical existence.[15]

2. Surmounting the Double Track of the Modern Mind

If in its discussion with the secular sciences Christian theology wants to surmount the double track of the modern mind (where it finds itself shunted off into a siding), there are certain things on which it must insist:

1. When theology disputes with the sciences, it is not wrestling only – and not mainly – for the soul of the scientist on the one hand, and, on the other, for the non-objectifiability of scientifically analysed and treated human beings. Theology's purpose cannot be reduced to the simple formula: 'the doctor as Christian' or 'the believing physicist'. Its true concern is the salvation of the world for which it hopes, and the calamity it fears; and because of that, it is interested not merely in the existence of the scientist as a man or woman, but also in the way scientists understand the world, and their scientific and practical dealings with reality. Here theology is not looking for a 'Christianized science' – and never for a clericalization of the university. What theology does do, however, is 'to represent the world for God and God for the world';[16] for it asks about *the future of the whole – its salvation or its doom –* which is won or thwarted in the historical process in which human beings and nature are mediated to each other.

The more world events become the world of history and society, the more pressing the question about the meaning, purpose and end of this process becomes. The more human beings have the power to make things possible, the more their powerlessness to know the 'why' and the 'where to' is exposed. Kant's question: 'What can I hope for?' crops up when, in the fear of possible disaster, the knowledge which is in itself limitless comes up against its limits. So it is impossible to separate world history from the event of salvation, for it is impossible to abandon to disaster the history which we create through our knowledge of nature and our technology. Hope for salvation and fear of disaster ultimately provide the driving power for human action. The question 'What can I hope for?' leads to reflection about the meaning of the question 'What can I know?', and the other question 'What should I do?' So it is not only the physicist and his possible victims that are relevant as a theological question. It is his physics itself. An understanding of the world in what we know and in what we do is not a matter of indifference in the Old or New Testaments, and not an arbitrary matter either. It we penetrate behind the ideas conditioned by their historical era, we find that it was in the sphere of behaviour towards the world especially that Israel wrestled passionately with the religions by which it was surrounded, just as Christianity did with Greek cosmology. In this dispute, Israel rejected the theophanous glorification of the world which elevated it into an image of the deity, and learnt to understand it as God's contingent creation, whose foundation was not in itself, and as an intrinsically open history of God's new, unforeseeable possibilities. In this dispute Christianity, by virtue of its hope for God's new creation, over-came both the Greek transfiguration of the cosmos (which saw it as the home of the world) and the Gnostic condemnation of the cosmos (which made it the worldly prison of the soul). In the era of history, for cosmos and the soul alike there is both peril and salvation. This perception led to reflection on temporal change: to an understanding of history in the light of its future, and to the experience of time, which unfurls itself out of its future. It was this which gave Greek thinking its turn from the static to the dynamic, from substance to function, from the blissful contem-plation of things as they are to their transformation in hope. And it is just such a dispute which the scientific and technological civilization of modern times imposes on Christian theology too.

But if theology is to acquire the openness for the world which is required, it is essential for it to emerge from a status in which it makes orthodox assertions about its own kind of truth, truth *sui generis,* and for it to develop a *theologia experimentalis*, an experimental theology which, together with the modern world, faces up to the *experimentum veritatis*, the experiment of truth. Theology must abandon its confinement to church, belief and the inwardness of the heart, so that with all others it may search for the truth of the whole, and the salvation of a torn and disrupted world.

2. Our term 'theology' originated in high scholasticism. There it means the scholarly or scientific presentation of the whole of Christian tradition, the *sacra doctrina*, or sacred teaching.[17] It derived its scientific character and its place in the comprehensive system of the sciences from its Aristotelian structure: the first philosophy – metaphysics – reached its highest point in theo-logic, the doctrine of God, which recounts the unity and totality in the construction of Being, and in the construction of know-ledge too. The God of Christian theology takes his name from history and the traditions of the Bible and the Church. But his universal deity is circumscribed with the aid of cosmological proofs of God's existence, and through Aristotelian metaphysics. The result is a harmony of biblical and philosophical theology. As the science of supreme Being and of ultimate value, Christian theology became an ordering power in the scientific cosmos.

This unity of theology and the sciences was shattered with the birth of modern times. There is no occasion for a romantic lament over 'the loss of the centre' for it was the loss of a fixed centre of this kind which led to the scientific disclosure of an endlessly rich wealth of ever-new horizons for the world. The God of the cosmological proofs of God could not suffice for the new horizons of an open, explorable and changeable world. This God became shadowy and obscure, ill-suited to act as working hypothesis for an explanation of the world. Nietzsche interpreted this process by asking: 'Who gave us the sponge to wipe out the whole horizon? What did we do when we unchained this earth from its sun?' But the question remained unanswered, and was more pressing than ever before: 'Where is it moving to now? Where are we moving to? Away from all the suns? Do we not continually stumble and fall? Backwards, sideways, forwards, in all directions? Is there still an above and a below? Are we not wandering through an infinite nothingness? Do we not feel the breath of empty space?'[18] So when the theological unity of reality and science which Aristotelian philosophy had formu-lated became antiquated, this by no means put an end to the question about unity and truth, and about the salvation and meaning of the whole. It was only now that for the first time this unity ceased to be the matter of course which tradition had made of it, and became an open question, which keeps the time and progress of human history in suspense, provoking ever new answers, and making of all the answers, answers that are super-seded and provisional. The truth and salvation of the whole is now understood in the form of an open question. As long as this question is open, and yet continues to present itself everywhere as a question, science remains science. 'A religion which without any hesitation declares war on reason cannot in the long run survive against it', declared Kant rightly.

And yet time has shown that in its enlightening victory over what it called faith, reason too did not stand simply on its own ground. It in fact developed highly unreasonable modes of naïve credulity. As Hegel rightly objected, 'Enlightened reason won a glorious victory over what it believed, in its limited conception of religion, to be faith opposed to reason. Yet seen in a clear light the victory comes to no more than this: the positive element with which reason busied itself to do battle, is no longer religion, and victorious reason in no longer reason. The new-born peace that hovers triumphantly over the corpse of reason and faith, uniting them as the child of both, has as little of reason in it as it has of authentic faith.'[19]

Ever since naïve scientific positivism – that curious child of rea-son and faith – started to break down, approaches have emerged at least two points for a new mutual understanding, and – over and above that – for a new community in theological and scien-tific thinking. These new points of approach can be found first in the problems about the foundations of science and theology, and second in the necessary development of an ethos for the scientific and technological domination of the world.

3. The Crisis of Scientific Foundations

As we know, positivism replaced the old, mythical and theologi-cal interpretation of the world by the recognition that there is a cohesion, subject to law, of all experiencable phenomena. But in this conviction it remained as naively credulous about Being as the theological epoch which it wanted to replace; for it assumed that reality was in itself exactly what scientific research showed it to be in its experiments. It believed in an absolute congruity between science and reality, and it considered the objective truth of scientific knowledge to be the absolute truth of Being. This meant that it was without history. It recognized neither the historicity of phenomena, nor the historicity of the observer, nor the historicity of the way phenomena and observer are mediated to each other in perception. Consequently it viewed the world it was able to discern and fashion, with all the solemnity appropriate to the ending of a mysterious, open history. Under its dominance, science became a magic word for the new world-magic, and was made the sole criterion for the knowledge of truth.

But Kant's critique of reason already showed 'that reason has insight only into that which it produces after a plan of its own, and that it must not allow itself to be kept, as it were, in nature's leading strings, but must itself show the way with principles of judgement based upon fixed laws, constraining nature to give answer to questions of reason's own determining'.[20] This means that the objective truth of science only becomes possible if reason has previously determined a horizon, a working draft, or a question, in which Being as object is brought to manifest itself under a particular aspect. Reason is constrained to remember that these are the conditions which make scientific objectivity possible. By a 'plan', project or working draft of this kind, Kant understood 'what [reason] itself has projected into nature'. The project therefore establishes the question which nature is constrained to answer, and excludes other questions as irrelevant. It also provides the context of meaning in which the nature which is subjected to enquiry becomes comprehensible, and where the observer can arrive at useful judgements. The objectivity of the perception and the judgement is therefore always dependent on the perspective from which a part of reality is observed. In an experiment, only the aspect where nature is constrained to answer the question put to it is brought forward in each given case. If the answer is to turn out to be clear and unambiguous, these aspects must always be artificial situations, abstract because of the limits they draw. The preparation for every experiment, every series of tests, and every questionnaire makes this clear: the criterion for the correctness of the results is their reproducibility, and that they prove to be identical when the experiment is repeated.

In its Hebrew root, 'thinking' always also means 'differentiating', and scientific thinking means excluding and screening out all the factors and aspects which are unimportant and inessential in a particular context.[21] Consequently the object of the investigation is prepared and the methods are considered beforehand. This methodological abstraction from other contexts and questions constitutes the scientific fascination with detail without which a science is impossible.

The so-called crisis in the foundations of modern physics, however, is due precisely to the fact that physics has come up against phenomena which can no longer be explained in the context of meaning which has been generally accepted up to now in classical physics. The phenomena themselves constrain the observer to consider the conditions and limitations of this traditional 'plan', outline or working draft. In the case of nuclear phenomena, the scientist is forced to view the outline of classical physics as one 'that can only be applied under certain conditions'. This gives us an insight into the hypothetical character of the working draft, which was formerly held to be universally applicable. So just at its most difficult point, nuclear physics, the hypothetical character of scientific perception has become evident. Scientific theories can no longer present themselves as being identical with the world as it really is. These theories are models – that is to say, observations within the limits set by the experiments. The old, still entirely metaphysical assumption of a world whose Being can be found within itself has therefore been replaced by what has been called 'the field of constructive possibilities'.[22] All that can be provided is not a picture of nature; it is a picture of certain relationships between the human being and nature. 'It has been realized that the scientific methods of separating, explaining and ordering have limits imposed on them, since the application of the methods changes and remodels their object, so that the methods can no longer be detached from that object, And in this way the scientific world picture ceases to be truly scientific.'[23]

The great 'world pictures' of the past are thus shown to be working drafts with whose help particular but limited experiences are possible. Successful experiment will show that the working drafts are correct. But to apply them to other phenomena makes us aware of the difference between reality and the mode of its appearance in the context of a particular question. Once there is clarity about this, the 'revolution in our ways of thinking' which Kant once heralded takes place in the sciences themselves. With some slight exaggeration the change can be expressed in this way: 'Is physics not an art (*techne*) rather than a science of Being – that is, an art of objectification? If this is so, exact science would not be a science of nature; it would rather be a science of an artificial nature created by human beings according to the idea of mathematics.'[24]

With an insight of this kind, science, constrained through its work on reality, itself moves away from the naïve, ontological shell of positivism and, realizing the hypothetical character of its outlines or working drafts, acquires a new understanding (a) of the inner interaction of method and object, (b) of the historicity of nature, and (c) of the fact that scientific reason is creative, and has the character of a historical working draft. Ideas and questions crop up which seem related to those of the humanities, for in the humanities the awareness that working drafts and methods are no more than perspectives is common coin, since the reality of human history is always complex.

In the human sciences analogous changes are more evident still. The image of the human being to which human life is made to conform has been replaced by the insight that any such image encompasses certain human phenomena. These images are models of limited range, variable, and always only applicable heuristically. Contemporary anthropological experiments teach us different aspects about human beings in each case.[25] The Russian biographer of Pavlov puts the following words into the mouth of the discoverer of conditioned reflexes: 'There we have it, the truth. We have shown that the "spiritual" is manageable. We can do with it whatever we want.'[26] It is already for scientific reasons, not just ethical ones, that the identification between the objective truth of a particular perspective and absolute truth has proved to be erroneous. It is an error about the conditions which make scientific objectivity possible. Objective truth remains objective truth; but it can be objectively proved that objective truth is not absolute truth; it is truth under certain conditions.[27] The world is not a machine just because machines can be made out of it, and the human being is not an aggregate of predetermined modes of social behaviour just because in a particular respect people may give the impression that this is so, and because their behaviour as consumers is calculable. Marxism confronts us over wide stretches with laws in nature and society which it has laid down with this kind of scientific positivism; but this is nothing but a grandiose relapse into a pre-critical age. With its insights into the necessity of the determination it affirms, it is itself a betrayal of the original dialectic of the historical process in which human beings and nature are mediated to each other, and which Marx made plain. Its materialistic, scientific credulity is the enemy of both history and human beings, as Marx himself rightly objected, in his criticism of the abstract materialism of the Enlightenment.

Whenever, then, we reflect self-critically in the way described about the conditions in which scientific statements are possible, we again set at liberty the possibility of enquiring about truth – about the truth and salvation of the whole, and about the true, whole and salutary condition of being human. Human beings become human whenever they ask the question about truth, and whenever they face up to it, for in the context of this question about the salvation and disaster of the world, freedom and responsibility become necessary. 'The true is the whole', said Hegel,[28] and the whole is the holy and the healed.

This brings us back to the meaning of this open question for science's knowledge of the world, and for the way it changes the world. 'The whole of reality' obviously eludes our grasp. Scientific knowing is compelled to restrict, to screen out, to exclude and abstract, if it wants to arrive at secure and well-founded knowledge. But what makes scientific reason aware of its limitations, and that its relations to the objects of its enquiry have the character of aspects? If it is always part-aspects that emerge, this leaves us with the question: part-aspects of what? For the self-critical reflection of reason cannot engender an agnostic relativism, and in the end a complete atomization of the sense of truth.

What kind of reality is it, which discloses itself to compulsive scientific elicitation, as the prelude to a successful domination of nature – a reality which in its totality still eludes scientific abstractions, so that the process of knowing finds no end? We can start with Goethe from the fact that this darkly mysterious wholeness of reality underlies all phenomena and all individual perceptions. 'In living nature nothing happens which is not connected with the whole, and even if experiences present themselves to us only in isolation – even if we have to view the experiments only as isolated facts – this does not mean that they are in fact isolated.' But if we note that the scientific knowledge and alteration of the world are themselves part of reality as well – that they do not merely confront it, but are also themselves an exorbitantly powerful element in the process of reality – then the other notion seems more convincing: the idea that the whole of reality is not only hidden, but is itself not yet *there* – that reality has not yet become rounded off into the whole, but is moving towards it, in an open history. This would mean that 'the whole' is not an eternal reality, for ever at the foundation of all its parts; reality is itself at stake in the process of history. The whole can be attained, but it can also be thwarted.[29] This, again, would mean that the whole is the future, the goal towards which reality is known, shaped, changed and processed. In fear and hope, in a world which becomes historical under our hands, we ask about the meaning and goal of this history, and in the face of possible disaster anticipate a salvation that has meaning for us.[30]

If 'the whole', then, is heralded out of the future of our historical world in the compelling necessity of the question about it, scientific knowing finds itself in a double process of knowing, one which moves in two contrary directions: it is forced to limit, screen out and abstract, in order to arrive at secure knowledge; but at the same time it is continually compelled to take its individual steps to knowledge in awareness of the reality of a whole that is still to come. That is to say, it has to be conscious of the scientific abstractions, and must at the same time lift and absorb them into a whole that is still ahead.[31] It is only where this uncertainty about the whole and the future thrusts itself on us that we become aware of our limitations and provisionality. The historical progress of scientific knowledge is kept on the move by the question which is always elusively ahead: the question about the truth and the future of the whole.

The vista of the open future in the process of the historical differentiation and mediation between subjectivity and objectivity, leads to a new state of reflection. Human beings no longer stand *over against* nature, as the determining subjects of knowledge and endeavour. As the determining subjects of knowledge and endeavour they are also part of a history *with* nature. They *have* nature – possess it – and yet they *are* themselves, at the same time, nature, which goes on developing in them and in their world. On the threshold of the open future which is ahead of nature together with human beings, and ahead of human beings together with nature, men and women will be conscious not only of their power over nature but also of their solidarity with it. The subject-object relationship between the subjectified human being and objectified nature becomes evident in the dialectical intertwining of the two. It itself has history and effects history.

The same insight puts a different face on reason. To see reason as a fully fledged and completed human capacity would clearly be to see it as too fixed and unmalleable. It is rather that reason itself assumes historical structures in the open play of working draft, experiment and reflection, since it itself moves towards truth in an openness in which truth is not already possessed, but which reason presupposes in the thought that reaches out to it in the working draft, without ever as yet fully capturing it. As long as the question of truth is still open, as a question about the salvation or disaster of the future, we are aware of the finite and provisional character of the working drafts. The human being finds no rest in his own blueprints and images, but with them voyages out into the open vista of the future.

4. The Theological Dimension of Science

It was an understandable misunderstanding when Christian theology took over the place that had been held by metaphysical *theo-logik* in the system of the sciences, and extolled the God of biblical history as the Unmoved Mover of the universe, or as the Supreme Being. It was an equally understandable misunderstanding when Christian theology surrendered its place where knowledge of the world is concerned, and withdrew to morality, inwardness and the Church's doctrine.

It is not only science which has emancipated itself from those metaphysics. The same can be said of theology. The sciences did so when they set out in the direction of horizons other than those illuminated by Greek cosmology. Theology did so when, in Pascal's words, it turned back to the God of Abraham, Isaac and Jacob, and the God of Christ's resurrection. Theology is therefore once more consciously 'Christian' theology. But in being so it ceases to draw its knowledge of the truth from a particular insight into the nature of 'the things that hold the world together in its innermost being'. It now derives its knowledge from the enduring recollection that Christ's cross and resurrection have brought into view 'the end of history' in God's future. The context of meaning in which the divine in the Christ event becomes comprehensible is not now the metaphysical framework; it is the eschatological one.[32] The universal significance of the *cross* of Christ is only understood in the context of judgement, the end-time crisis of all things; and the *resurrection* of Christ from the dead is only understood in the context of a universal transformation, whose future is the kingdom of God. It is in the light of this future that the coming of Christ takes on meaning. But conversely, it is through his coming that awareness of a universal end of history has entered the world of the nations.

Ever since then, this ultimate future of crisis and salvation has been the 'soul' of time, thought of historically. The question about the end of history is the question about the significance of the historical and social world for the expectations that guide action; for action is always an expecting in fear or hope.[33]

This means that Christianity is neither 'metaphysics for the educated' nor 'Platonism for the people', as Nietzsche put it. It is a universal hope for the future which embraces the history of human beings and the history of the world. The Christ event of the resurrection is 'historical' in that it confers history by opening up new future: through this event of the past – which is nevertheless not a past event – the present is thrown open for the future, as a time of hope. Theological knowledge of the truth springs from the perception of this unique happening; but it can only perceive the meaning of this event by understanding it against the horizon of the future which this event throws ahead of itself, and which it heralds. Theological knowledge of the truth can consequently be called historical, and in being historical it also anticipates the universal future. The more we contemplate the Christ event through remembrance, the more compellingly we call to mind the open future of the world. Through this remembrance, theological perception of the coming truth of the whole in the Christ event becomes aware that its own perception is no more than provisional. So it does not have a supernatural character. It has the character, peculiarly its own, of being the remembering knowledge of hope. Consequently it will also put the unique stamp of the provisional and the open on human beings' knowledge of nature and themselves.

The fullness of all things – that whole of reality – is not concealed behind some backcloth to the world. For the Christian hope, the fullness of all things and times is set in the fulfilment of what is promised, and in what is therefore historically open here and now. The phrase Paul uses, 'that God may be all in all' (1 Cor. 15.23), does not mean the eternal presence of Being (which is what it would have meant for the Stoics). It means the future goal of all things which are here involved in history.

If in the historical Christ event Christian theology thinks about 'the end of history' – if it therefore sees the world and human beings exposed to the interplay of crisis and salvation – it will no longer be able to separate its supernatural from its natural knowledge. It will set natural knowledge within the open question of the ultimate future. God's revelation in Christ has to be understood as the opening up of a world history in which the future of salvation is at stake. This does not merely open men and women in the religious perspective of the human heart; the opening means an opening in all the perspectives where men and women try to make sure of themselves, and of nature and society. Christian theology can no longer remain obstinately entrenched over against the sciences. Together with the sciences, it enters the front or interface we call the present, where the future will be either won or thwarted, because the salvation of the world is hoped for and disaster feared. So theological reflections of this kind are not the prerogative of one special university faculty among others. They belong to the horizon of perception for every scientific discipline.

What we are pursuing in our theological faculties is really *pastoral* theology. The professional purposes for which theology is needed have been reduced to the requirements of priest or pastor, or those responsible for religious education in schools. These purposes, for which 'one needs' theology, also determine the character and build-up of the subject: from exegesis to preaching, to instruction, to pastoral care and counselling. Today a new lay theology is developing outside the theological faculties, which is notable theologically but also practically and as a scientific discipline. If the universities want to meet the challenge of these changed conditions, this lay theology must be institutionalized in non-theological faculties, in the form of departments or the like.

The horizons against which reality can be disclosed to science reflect the restricted, finite and historically provisional horizons of our knowledge. The end of history, which Christian theology is talking about whenever it talks about Christ, is like an ultimate horizon which moves with us, and continually invites us to follow it further.[34] For truth and salvation are not accessible to theology either as something that can be possessed, but only in the form of faith and hope. Theology knows the ultimate meaning which the future of history can give only in the mode of expectation. But hope, which is guided by the prevenient anticipation of the future, exposes itself to the *experimentum veritatis* – the experiment of truth. If hope is not merely directed towards the possible consequences of action and its successes, but reaches out beyond everything visible and possible to a meaning for *everything* that happens here, then that is a hope on which certainty is conferred in the face of total uncertainty: 'Death, where is thy sting? Grave, where is thy victory?' (1 Cor. 15.55 AV).[35]

Theology will communicate to the spirit which is at work in the modern sciences its own unrest: 'Now we see through a mirror in a dark word (Luther's translation), but then face to face. Now I know in part, but then I shall know even as I am known' (1 Cor. 13.12).

But the modern sciences will compel Christian theology to adopt the new stance which Pierre Teilhard de Chardin described: 'Earlier there seemed to be only two geometrically possible attitudes for men and women: to love heaven or to love the earth. Here a third way is emerging: to pass through the earth on the way to heaven. There is a community, the true community – with God through the world.'[36]

On the other hand, theology and science are now encountering one another at a more fundamental level than ever before, as both face the question about the ethos of the technological acquisition of the power given by scientific knowledge, and the responsibility that power involves. The time is irrevocably past when scientists could withdraw with a clear conscience into their laboratories, ignoring the demands of the time. The finer the commitment to scientific objectivity in research, and the more successful the work, the more urgent the need for the ethical and political responsibility for humanity and world history which has hitherto been excluded. Modern science is indissolubly bound up with the potentialities of modern technology. These in their turn depend on the investments which have to be made in 'big science' and national planning by society as a whole. Investments of this kind are only useful if the projects they promote are searching for the future of a life of human dignity. Here interdependencies are obvious – with politics, with the social order, and with visions of the future; and these have to be taken into account.

Scientific work has initially to detach itself from questions of this kind which affect the whole. For a long time the exactness of the methods used was also the quintessence of the scientist's ethical training. This had all the beauty of an end in itself. But now, in face of the unforeseeable potentialities and the unforeseeable consequences of the scientific acquisition of power, we must go beyond this, and ask about the purpose and meaning of this power for the whole. Science acquired its power by abstracting itself from world history. But for that very reason it has acquired – often without knowing what was happening – an immense amount of power over this world. Disinterested commitment to the subject in hand therefore engendered a responsibility which requires a new ethos that goes beyond pure objectivity. Einstein once said that earlier, people had perfect purposes but highly imperfect means of achieving them; today we have perfect means and immense possibilities, but confused purposes.

If ideas about values are so arbitrary and hence so confused, what are the standards by which we should judge the results of value-free science? How should we arrive at the best decisions if we are not clear about what is best? Science and scientific technology have changed the world. This change becomes crucial where the essential point is not just to know and to be informed, but also to decide what should be done. For science has to screen out the questions about the 'why' and 'to what end'. But that does not mean that these questions are obsolete just because they are unscientific. They revert to us again with unsuspected urgency. Science 'teaches us methods, but it doesn't teach us what we should do', said Dippel. 'The God of physics is there to give us what we want', said Santillana, 'but not to tell us what we *ought* to want.'[37]

Initially, human beings were dependent on obscure and mysterious forces in nature and history. Then they saw through these forces, and were able to explain their laws and conditions. History that had been suffered without awareness thus became history that was perceived as such. That was the first Enlightenment. Today we recognize that we have been liberated from these forces. We can now master them. But through that very fact, human beings have become dependent in a new way. They are now dependent on their own works. Processes were set going which, as they developed, evolved their own laws over which human beings are no longer master. Their own products are too much for them. They are unable to rid themselves again of the spirits they have conjured up. The first Enlightenment wanted to know and understand what had previously been uncomprehendingly suffered. The new Enlightenment must become an Enlightenment of the Enlightenment:[38] we must consciously shape and bring under human control the power that was earlier unconsciously and disinterestedly captured.

Today the old divorce between theory and practice, science and politics can no longer be implemented. Theories about science are acquiring practical significance, and practice is everywhere theorized. This interweaving of theory and practice has always been recognized in every science which has directly practical consequences. In medicine, the Hippocratic oath was – and was intended to be – the subject of reflection, because in medicine the human being is not merely the object of research, but is always at the same time the life itself which has to be preserved and furthered. On a larger scale, this interplay is obvious today in all the sciences, from nuclear physics to biogenetics. It showed itself compellingly in the inner conflicts which Einstein and Oppenheimer suffered during their work on the atomic bomb.[39] In 1957, the awareness of the interplay was formulated by eighteen German nuclear physicists in the Göttingen Declaration, where they documented their refusal to co-operate in the nuclear arming of the Federal Republic's armed forces. Unfortunately the reaction was merely to reiterate the age-old separation of competences: the political consequences of their scientific work was said to be outside the scientists' area of responsibility. This set off a discussion about the introduction of a professional oath for scientists.[40] It is true that no oath would be able to prevent misuse today, for divided humanity is still a long way from ethical solidarity where its responsibility for the scientific acquisition of power is concerned. But the necessity cannot be lightly rejected; for it is only in the shared growth of mutual trust, reciprocal supervision, and democratic controls of the controllers that this responsibility can be implemented.

Without abstraction from world history we cannot learn anything scientifically; but this detachment must continually be absorbed into the responsibility of human beings for the whole. Technological reason must be freed from ethical, practical reason, but must at the same time be integrated into it. It is only in their continual interplay that the two can grow from one another. Taken by itself, technological reason offers no criteria for the goodness of what can be done with it. Taken by itself, ethical reason has no means with which it can fulfil its purposes. It is only in continual dialogue that these two things can be mediated to each other – on the one hand technological power, and on the other the future goals of a hope for humanity which lends meaning to the whole.

Up to now Christian theology has assented to the age-old division of competences, and has made a clear cut between the realm in which the world is to be preserved and shaped, and its own realm of salvation. But the future of the salvation on which it sets its hopes is the future of the whole, which as time goes by is increasingly involved in the risk of human history; and once theology recognizes this, it must betake itself to the intermediate realm between the sustaining of the world and its final consummation.[41] It must mediate between the ultimate future of crisis and salvation, and the historical goals of human endeavour, so that this world may be discerned and changed in the light of God's final promises. Like disaster too, the future of salvation never lies before us, finished and without a history, so that we could submit to it either fatalistically or in carefree confidence. It always already takes form in the historical movement which is underway towards it, so that it is only when we search for that future that we shall be able to find it.

Max Weber closed his famous lecture on 'Science as a Vocation' by pointing out that for the people 'who await new prophets and saviours the situation is the same as that which echoes through the beautiful Edomite watchman's song which has found a place in the Isaiah oracles, from the period of the Exile: "There comes a cry from Seir in Edom: Watchman, how long still the night? The watchman answers: the morning cometh but it is still night. If you will enquire, come another time."'[42] But if theology vouches for God to the world and for the world before God, what it sees over the world is not just night. It must rouse all its senses in expectation of the coming morning. It must sharpen the sense of responsibility and the ability to look ahead, in all the different disciplines. For the hour in which theology is living can be described in Paul's words: 'The night is far gone, the day is at hand' (Rom. 13.12). It is only together with the sciences that eschatological faith can arrive at confidence in history.

II

Theologians and Scientists on the Way to Wisdom

What are the areas where science and religion can meet? Where can they engage in a fruitful dialogue aiming at a co-operation which will further life?

Up to now the attempt to bring *pure science and scientific, or scholarly, theology* into direct dialogue has borne only limited fruits. For this there are two main reasons. For one thing, scientists do not expect this dialogue to bring them any increase of knowledge in their own field. For another, many scientists, and a good many theologians too, lack the knowledge of philosophy which would provide a mediating level. Often enough terms are used which have not been critically thought through, so they cannot be made comprehensible. I remember a discussion with astrophysicists during which someone suggested using the word 'multiverse' instead of universe, but was uncertain whether the term ought to be a singular or a plural. I am also thinking of theologians who have never read a scientific book because they don't believe that any such book could teach them anything about the wisdom of God. 'The book of nature' has long since ceased to be studied by theologians of Holy Scripture.

Mediating levels for a fruitful interaction between science and scientific theology could perhaps be found in a comprehensive philosophical epistemology or theory of knowledge, or in a general hermeneutics of history; for these could take in and integrate both experiences of nature and experiences of transcendence.[1]

Another attempt tries to relate *science and religion* to each other quite directly. This approach is promoted by the John Templeton Foundation in the United States. It accommodates the scientists who think religiously about their own specialist field and beyond it, without pinning them down to a particular religion or the dogma of any one faith. It is only seldom that a theologian meets the corresponding requirement of having thought about science on the basis of his theology, and beyond it.[2] Theologians of this kind have become increasingly rare ever since the Enlightenment, and today they are almost an extinct race. In this sphere too it is difficult to find the mediations which would make a fruitful co-operation possible. The scientist experiences nature through observation and experiment. It is hard to bring this experience into harmony with the religious experience of nature: the one is objective and repeatable, the other subjective and unrepeatable; the one is universal, the other communal. Yet we use the same word 'experience' for both. Could this broad and ambiguous term 'experience' [3] provide a mediating level for the general and the particular, for what is subject to law and for what is contingent?

The approaches which enjoy the greatest popularity today try to *relate the sciences directly to ethics*. For the last thirty years at least, German universities have had chairs and commissions for 'ethics in the sciences' and working parties for 'the assessment of the results of technology'. Medically applied sciences have provoked an ethics of life and an appreciation of the patient as person. The biogenetic and biotechnical progress of recent years has led to the establishment of 'ethical councils' at every level of political decision. The aim of these councils is to regulate the use of biotechnical power over life, and to make it accountable to the humane values of society. But because 'freedom of research' is premised but never discussed, ethical reflections are always too late on the scene.[4] Scientific research is objective, but it is not value free. It is subjected to the utilitarian interests of society. Today freedom for scientific research on human embryos is forcibly driven forward by the capitalist competitive principle. Society's assent is now and again extorted through the argument that what we don't do here, other people will do somewhere else, and that we shall then be left behind in the race for scientific and technological achievement. The inherent ethos of scientific and technological progress has its own dynamic, both factual and fictitious, of the do-able and the illusory. This dynamic is so powerful that every humane ethics which is introduced only after this power has been employed is helpless. The old advancement optimism has been replaced, not by pessimism but by fatalism. This advancement fatalism really permits no ethical alternatives. Every policy capitulates before the dictatorship of science and technology, and 'deregulates' them, so that it can withdraw from this sector altogether. But then who protects the cherished 'freedom for research' (which is enshrined in the German constitution) from economic pressures?

This means that we have to go further, and see the modern sciences, and especially the biosciences, in their economic and social context. And this context is the scientific-technological-industrial complex of modern society. We must then go on to ask: is science in good keeping within this complex? And is this complex itself wisely organized – that is to say, in a way that furthers life? On the other hand, ethics cannot be reduced to absolute values and obligations either. They receive their *Sitz im Leben* – their real-life situation – from the tradition, culture and religion of modern society. Here too we are faced with questions about the wisdom and life-furthering quality of this cultural complex of modern times.

A new attempt to see science and theology in the context of the life common to them both is made on the level of *wisdom*. According to the tradition of the ancient world, all knowledge is embedded in wisdom about life. The Greek word *phronesis* embraces both knowledge and morality, so that people learn how to deal wisely with what they know, and how to relate their morality realistically to the reality perceived. Not all knowledge furthers life – not every perception makes us wise. We become wise from experience, good and bad. In the learning process of life and death we become wise to the extent to which we remain interested in life. It was the modern scientific revolution which for the first time detached the sciences from this context, and interpreted scientific reason as 'instrumental reason' – as a way to power over nature and our own lives.[5] If knowledge is nothing but power, as Francis Bacon taught, and if science is nothing but methods of seizing power over some part of nature, then our capacity for acquiring new knowledge will increasingly come to outrun our capacity for using this power wisely. The emancipation of the sciences from moral philosophy and theology was in reality their emancipation from wisdom.[6]

But what is meant by an all-embracing wisdom?

Let us first look at theology, and ask about its relation to wisdom, and what it understands by wisdom. In the degree to which reason emancipated itself from wisdom, theology took leave of it as well, and tried to arrive at its own self directly. Over against emancipated reason, it tried to base itself wholly and exclusively on the self-revelation of God, or the self-assurance of faith. The conflict between 'reason and revelation' led to a dispute between the faculties and within theology itself about the rights and wrongs of 'natural theology'. If we look into this internal theological dispute impartially, we discover that there cannot in fact be any rivalry between revelation theology and natural theology. A natural knowledge of God perceives God as the creator and sustainer of the world indirectly or by way of analogy from creation and the course of the world; and through perception it creates a community with what it perceives, as every perception does. Through natural theology people become *wise* in their dealings with nature; but they would not be saved. Salvation is given only through perception of the revelation of God the redeemer. But if people were to cling exclusively to this revelation of God, and were not to concede any natural knowledge of him, they would be saved but not wise.

It follows from this old traditional difference that the category natural theology (*theologia naturalis*) is in reality a practical wisdom (*sapientia practica*); it is not theology in the modern sense. Revelation theology would lose its context in life and in the lived reality of nature if it were to surrender the teachings of natural wisdom. Faith and reason can find each other in the house of wisdom they share, and each of them can contribute its own insights to the building of this house in a culture based on wisdom about life.[7] On the theological side, it was always the task of natural theology, or a theology of nature, to discover and learn wisdom of this kind, which is in accord with the God of revelation and faith. In the seventeenth century, the aim of what was called physico-theology was to acquire this wisdom in the spheres of the new sciences, and this theology has to be understood as sapiential. A famous book of the time (it was first published in 1672) was John Ray's *The Wisdom of God Manifested in the Works of Creation*.

In seeking wisdom we discover and we learn. We discover an already given wisdom in the build-up of matter and the stages of organic life. Molecular combinations and cell organisms that further life have come into being, while others, hostile to life, have been excluded. What in our one-sided, linear thinking we call evolution, is really a complex learning process on the part of the living. The genetic code is capable of learning, and is creative. In the build-up of matter and life, a primordial *memory* is stored which well deserves the name 'wisdom'. The human species was only a latecomer on the blue planet, earth. It therefore has every reason to enquire about the wisdom of the living and their ecosystems, so as to learn from them its own 'worldly wisdom'. We need scientific observations and experiments, not just for the purpose of gathering information, but also in order to learn from the wisdom which is inherent in nature.

But if science's knowledge-constitutive question – the question that prompts its investigations – is merely to discover what we can 'do' with the object perceived, or how it can be changed and made of utility for human beings, the search for wisdom stops. This is interventionist science. It puts an end to astonishment (*thaumazein*) over the phenomena, and replaces wonder by cost-benefit calculations. We can see this from the fact that more and more biological findings – for example the deciphering of the human genome – are immediately patented, so that they can be sold for profit. One-sided human domination stupefies nature and makes human beings stupid.

But if the predetermined intention is the search for human

wisdom about life, then research is guided by other interests. Then a dialogue emerges between the natural wisdom that has been discovered and the human wisdom that has to be learnt. Human wisdom will search for viable harmonizations between human civilization and the earth's ecosystems. Then the goal is not human domination over nature; it is a well-judged and prudent conformity with nature.[8] It begins with respect for the primordial *memory of life* embedded in the natural processes, and with what Albert Schweitzer called reverence for life, as the foremost commandment which follows from the right to life.

THEOLOGY AND COSMOLOGY

III

Creation as an Open System

1. Two Problems

1. As we know, the beginning of the modern era brought with it a crisis in the relationship between science and belief in creation. The sciences emancipated themselves from the religious culture of the middle ages and inaugurated the secular culture of modern times. Theology became apologetic, and merely fought rearguard battles against the triumphal progress of the sciences, either limiting belief in creation deistically to the original contingency of the universe,[1] or restricting it existentially to the personal contingency of human existence.[2] Either that, or it cut off its Church dogmatics from the sciences in such a way that the two neither interfered with each other, nor had anything to say to each other at all.[3] In its intention to co-exist with the sciences, theology itself deepened the rift it wanted to overcome. Today we are trying to find a convergence between science and belief in creation; but the precondition for this attempt is, on the one hand, a rethinking of theology's traditional concept of creation and, on the other, a revision of the concept of nature held by classical science. The ecological crisis caused by the progressive destruction of nature has been brought about by Christianity and science jointly; and if human beings and nature want to win a chance to survive in the face of this crisis, Christianity and science must together revise their picture of the human being – both the view reflected in the traditional belief in creation ('subdue the earth', Gen. 1.28), and the view held in Cartesian science, according to which the human being is '*maître et possesseur de la nature*'.

2. Christian dogmatics developed in the framework of Greek thinking, and ever since, theological method has always started with an account of the world's creation, only arriving at the idea of the world's redemption last of all. Because of this way of thinking, redemption has always been related to creation, and understood from that perspective. The creation of the world was really the foundation for everything. In the beginning was God the Creator, and his creation was very good, perfect and complete. At the end everything will be again as it was at the beginning – τὰ ἔσχατα ὡς τὰ πρῶτα – Redemption is then nothing but the restitution of the original, goodly creation: *restitutio in integrum* – a restoration of the beginning.

If we see redemption in this way, from the perspective of creation and for the sake of creation, we have a *protological understanding of eschatology*. In that case, history between creation and redemption is primarily the history of the Fall. It cannot bring anything new – only the increasing deterioration and obsolescence of what was once created. Only redemption will restore creation. Today, in my view, the doctrine of creation has to be revised, first for exegetical reasons, and second because of our own experiences, and our own dealings with nature. And this revision means turning things upside down and arriving at an *eschatological understanding of creation*. Then eschatology is no longer seen only in the light of creation; creation is also understood in the light of eschatology.[4]

2. Is Creation a Closed System or an Open One, and in What Respect?

The final syllable of the German word for creation, *Schöpfung*, indicates the *completed* process of creative activity and its result. Consequently when we talk about creation, we instinctively think, theologically speaking, about the original state of the world and the beginning of all things, imagining them as a condition that was once finished, complete in itself and perfect. Belief in creation echoes the Creator's judgement over his creation: 'Behold, it was very good.'

Unfortunately we cannot, like our Creator, come to rest at this point. For experience tells us: 'Behold, it is unfortunately not very good at all.' It has been spoilt; it is 'corrupt', says the Bible (Gen. 6.5, 11). This discrepancy between the judgement of faith and the judgement of experience has led people to place the 'very good' creation ahead of history, and to describe it with religious symbols of origin as an image of religious memory. Dogma called Adam's condition in paradise the *status integritatis* – the pure and perfect state. As the one whose creation was 'very good', Adam possessed the primal righteousness and sanctity (*iustitia et sanctitas originalis*). The first man and woman were driven out of this perfect state because of their sin. And to this perfect state redemption will lead them back.

So what is history? It is first of all paradise lost, and then the road to exile. And what is redemption? It is the way back home and, at last, as the final outcome, paradise regained. Sin perverts the good creation. Grace restores it. What emerges at the end of this history of sin and grace is the good creation as it originally was and always is. In the history of religion this pattern corresponds to 'the myth of the eternal return' described by Mircea Eliade.[5] Did Thomas Aquinas mean anything different when he said: 'The end of things corresponds to their beginning: after all, God is the beginning and end of all things. Therefore the emergence of things from their beginning corresponds to their return to their end'?[6] At all events, for Aquinas time has a symmetrical, circular structure.[7]

Did Rudolf Bultmann too mean anything different when he wrote: 'No light shone in Jesus other than the light that always shone in creation. In the light of the revelation of redemption, the human being does not have to understand himself any differently from the way he was always supposed to understand himself in the face of revelation in creation and law: as God's creation.' At all events, for Bultmann too time has a symmetrical, circular structure: 'So what meaning has the divine righteousness or the forgiveness of sins? . . . Its meaning is that the original relationship of creation will be restored.'[8]

According to what the wording would seem to suggest, as

well as the traditional interpretations, original creation is non-historical. History begins only with the Fall, and ends when creation is restored in the redemption. Creation itself has neither time nor history. The picture of creation which is projected in this way is the picture of a closed system, perfect in itself and totally self-sufficient.

But modern Old and New Testament exegesis will not allow us to maintain this notion of creation. Biblically, belief in creation is determined by faith in salvation, as a historical process; and since faith in salvation as a historical process is determined by redemption, eschatology also determines the experience of history and belief in creation. As systematically important findings of Old Testament exegesis we may mention the following:

1. The Israelite belief in creation developed out of Israel's experience of God in history – the exodus, the covenant, the occupation of the promised land – and was moulded by this experience. Israel had a 'soteriological understanding of the work of creation'.[9]

2. In both the Yahwist and the Priestly Writing, creation in the beginning does not mean an unscathed primal condition; it means the history that precedes salvation history. That is why creation with its various orders is itself understood as the work of Yahweh's grace, and is narrated in the form of the *toledoth*, or genealogy. With creation in the beginning 'There is a real and true opening up of historical prospect'.[10] God's history with the world does not just begin after the Fall; it begins with creation. Creation is aligned towards the future, so we can say: 'In Old Testament theology creation is an eschatological concept.'[11]

3. The information: 'In the beginning God created' establishes time together with creation. But if time begins simultaneously with 'creation in the beginning', then creation must be subject to change from the beginning, for time is only perceived from alteration. But if creation is from the beginning subject to change and open to time, then it cannot be a closed system; it can only be an open one. Consequently the time that begins with creation does not have a symmetrical structure either – a structure in which future and past, goal and origin correspond, like the two

halves of a circle. Time's structure is a-symmetrical. It is open for
a future which does not have to be the return of what was at the
beginning, in the form of a *restitutio in integrum*, a restoration
of the original condition. Some scholars have thought that 'creation in the beginning' already envisages the consummation of
creation 'at the end', because the idea of *acharith* (end) and the
idea of *reshith* (beginning) belong together.[12] Even if this cannot
be deduced directly from the concept 'in the beginning', according to the Priestly Writing creation at the beginning does point
forward towards 'God's resting', and, according to the Yahwist,
towards the universal fulfilment of the blessing to Abraham.
These determinations of a goal may be termed eschatological. 'To the beginning there corresponds an end; to creation
there corresponds a consummation; to the "very good" here a
"perfectly glorious" there.'[13]

It follows from this that theology must talk about creation not
only at the beginning, but also in history and at the end. That is
to say, in what we say we have to have in view the total process
of divine creative activity. 'Creation' as the quintessence of
God's creative activity comprehends creation at the beginning,
the creations of history, and the creation of the End-time. It
embraces the initial creative activity, creative activity in history,
and the eschatological consummation. The reduction of the
concept of creation to creation in the beginning has led traditionally either to the rift between 'creation and redemption' and
between 'nature and super-nature', or to a cleavage between 'the
first and the second creation'. But this calls in question the
continuity and unity of the divine creative activity itself. The concept of the unity of God in the unity of meaning of his creative
activity can, in my view, only be preserved through the concept
of the coherent, eschatologically orientated process of creation.
If this is correct, then the position of human beings with regard
to creation changes as well. The human being no longer merely
confronts God's non-human creation as the creature made in the
image of God, and creation's lord; now, together with all other
living things, he belongs within the Becoming of creation's still
open, uncompleted process. Creation is then not a *factum* but a

fieri – not just made, but also to-be-made. This leads to a new interpretation of human destiny in creation; and 'subdue the earth' cannot be that destiny's final word.

If theology wants to give a summary account of God's creative activity, it must then view creation as the still open, creative process of reality. To put it in traditional terms, we mean by this the unity of the *regnum naturale* (the kingdom of nature), the *regnum gratiae* (the kingdom of grace) and the *regnum gloriae* (the kingdom of glory), each viewed in eschatological perspective. The initial creation points towards salvation history, and both point beyond themselves to the kingdom of glory. It is not the covenant of grace which already provides the 'inner ground' for creation in the beginning; the inner ground is given only with the kingdom of glory. For the kingdom of glory is the inner motivation of the divine history of the covenant. At the same time, in the process of creation which is wholly aligned towards glory, we can distinguish between the following, according to their different conditions:

(a) creation in the beginning;
(b) the creations of history;
(c) the creation of the End-time.

3. Creation in the Beginning

According to the texts, creation in the beginning is evidently creation without any presuppositions. *Creatio ex nihilo*, creation out of nothing (*ouk on*, 'nothingness' being meant, and not *me on*, 'non-being', to use Platonic language) is an expression intended to convey the liberty of the Creator and the contingency of all being – both its initial contingency and the contingency that is permanent and fundamental. The question: Why is there something rather than nothing? cannot be answered by pointing to any necessity. But it cannot be answered by pointing to pure chance either. *Creatio ex nihilo* defines in a negative way the positive ground of creation in God's good pleasure. Out of 'the inner necessity of his love', to use Barth's phrase, the Creator creates something that corresponds to him and gives him pleasure. That is why in its contingency creation has a meaning. This is the reason why it is pleasurable and lovable beyond 'chance and necessity', as Jacques Monod puts it.[14]

Creation in the beginning is simultaneously the creation of time. It must therefore be understood as *creatio mutabilis,* a creation that is subject to change. It is perfectible, not perfect, for it is open for the history of both disaster and salvation, for both corruption and consummation. If we understand creation individually and as a whole as *an open system*, then its beginning is at the same time the condition for its history and its completion.[15] The creation at the beginning is the creation of conditions for the potentialities of creation's history. It pegs out the experimental field of constructive and destructive possibilities. It is open for time and for its own alteration in time. We cannot see in it the invariant nature of history, but we can see the beginning of the history of nature.

The creation accounts tell us that the initial creation *out of* chaos is also a creation of order *in* chaos. In the symbolic language of the Bible, the forces of chaos – night and the sea – thrust themselves into creation, even though they are excluded and confined by God. *Creatio ex nihilo* (creation out of nothing) is therefore also *creatio in nihilo* (creation into nothing). It is consequently creation that is threatened, and only protected to a limited degree against that threat. In the apocalyptic visions of the creation of the End-time, in contrast, the encroaching forces of chaos are absent (Rev. 21.1; 22.5). The creation of glory is to be a creation that is no longer threatened and no longer vulnerable. In that creation God will be 'all in all' (1 Cor. 15.28 AV), for then his glory will evidently interpenetrate everything, overcoming not only destruction but even the possibility of destruction, not just death but even the possibility of death. The Augustinian doctrine of freedom says the same thing: the initial *posse non peccare* (I am able not to sin) is to be overcome by the *non posse peccare* (I am unable to sin) of the End-time, and the initial *posse non mori* (I am able not to die) by the End-time's *non posse mori* (I cannot die). The inference is that human beings

were created as 'potentiality *for*'. They are certainly destined for
righteousness and not for sin, and for glory, not death. But they
can still miss the mark of what they are potentially destined for.
This cannot be termed what Barth calls an 'impossible possibility'
in the ontological sense; but it can in the ethical sense be called a
possibility which ought not to be realized.

4. Creative Acts in History

In ascribing to Israel a soteriological understanding of creation in
the beginning, we must also, conversely, recognize that Israel had
an understanding of salvation in history which was based on
creation. The prophets use *bara,* the word for creating without
presuppositions, more frequently for the divine creation of new,
unexpected and unmerited salvation in history than for creation
in the beginning. Like the Psalms, the prophets saw the exodus
and the creation of the world, the creation of the world and the
exodus of the End-time as belonging within a single perspective.
Consequently belief in creation also ministers to faith in salvation, because for faith in salvation, salvation issues from God's
new creations. That is why creation in the beginning can be
extolled as an act of salvation, and the redemption can be
expected in terms of a new creation.

The creation events of history are God's free acts, and hence
contingent. But, unlike creation in the beginning, they are not
without preconditions. They are depicted as the creation of something new out of something old – of salvation out of wretched-
ness and life from dead bones. The divine creating at the beginning is conceived of as an effortless creating through the Word;
but the divine creating of redemption is understood as God's
weariness and labour (Isa.43.24; Isa. 53). The creating of salvation for those who are without it, issues from the suffering of
God's love for his people. Because Israel understood itself as
being exemplary for the nations and for the whole of creation,
we can view its experience of history as exemplary for the understanding of history in general. Here the hidden actions of God in
history are manifested in an exemplary way.

To what are God's creative acts in history related? Theological language relates salvation to sin and sickness, and redemption to enslavement. But what are sin and enslavement? Having called creation in the beginning a system open for time and potentiality, we can understand sin and enslavement as the self-closing of open systems against their own time and their own potentialities.[16] If people close themselves against their own potentialities, they tie themselves down to their present reality; they are trying to endorse their present, and to keep hold of it in the face of possible changes. The person who does this turns into *homo incurvatus in se:* he will be turned in on himself, and become the image of Narcissus in the myth. If a human society settles down as a closed system, seeking to be self-sufficient, something similar happens: a society of this kind will extend its own present into the future, and will merely confirm the form it has already acquired. For that society the future loses its scope for possible changes; and in this way the society surrenders its freedom. A society of this kind is turned in on itself too; it becomes a *societas incurvata in se.* This is what Christopher Lasch calls 'the culture of narcissism'. Natural history demonstrates from other living things as well that closing up against the future, self-immunization against change, and the breaking-off of communication with other living things leads to self-destruction and death. Although isolation in individuals and human society can hardly be compared with other phenomena (since human beings and societies have their own special destinies), analogous phenomena can be shown in other living things too. Whereas the word 'sin' only means human misdemeanour, the concept of deadly self-isolation can lead to the fuller understanding of the 'subjection of the whole creation to futility' which Paul talks about in Rom. 8.19ff.

If in history God creates salvation for the people that lacks it, this means that he liberates that people from enslavement, whether it is self-imposed or imposed from outside. If he creates grace for the sinner, this means that he frees that sinner from his or her self-isolation. We can therefore call salvation in history the divine opening of 'closed systems'. The closed or isolated person is freed for freedom and thrown open for his or her own future (Gal. 5.1). A closed society is brought to life so that it can look upon and act towards the future as being the transformation of itself. Non-human life systems enter into communication with each other once more. But because closed or isolated systems can only be opened again by means of renewed communication with others, if they are not to be destroyed, the opening to God comes about through God's suffering over their isolation. Because God himself suffers over humanity's closedness towards him, he keeps his communication with human beings alive in spite of opposition, creating through his faithfulness the domain where isolated men and women can open and transform themselves.[17] The openness of human beings to God is therefore brought about by grace, and grace springs from the suffering of God's love for isolated human beings.

The opening of a closed human society for openness for neighbourliness and towards nature can be thought of analogously. Closed systems bar themselves against suffering and self-transformation. They grow rigid and condemn themselves to death. The opening of closed systems and the breaking down of their barriers and immunizations will have to come about through the acceptance and assumption of suffering. But the only living beings that are capable of this are the ones which display a high degree of vulnerability and capacity for change – that is to say, the ones that are free. They are not merely alive; they can make other things come alive as well.

Anyone who looks for statements about creation in the New Testament often finds the results disappointing. Apart from the beautiful 'lilies of the field', creation doesn't seem to be a new theme. But we only get this impression if we are looking for statements about creation in the beginning. The New Testament testimony to creation is embedded in the kerygma about the resurrection, and in pneumatology. There God's creative activity is understood eschatologically as καλεῖν (call to life), as ἐγείρειν (raise) and as ζωοποιοῦν (make alive), for they are related to the creation of the End-time, that is 'the new creation'.[18]

For Paul, with the raising of the Christ who had been surrendered to death the creation of the End-time begins. He describes this creation as a process which has begun with the raising of Christ, which continues to be efficacious in the revelation of the Spirit, and which will be perfected with the quickening of mortal bodies – that is to say, the resurrection of the dead. For Paul, the perfect tense of the resurrection of Christ always points to the future tense of our own resurrection and the new creation of all things. When in certain passages he talks about an order in this process (1 Cor. 15.20ff.), he does not mean that the parts are separate from one another. He makes the unified character of the process of the new creation clear through the concept of *aparche,* 'the first fruits'.[19]

When quickening and resurrection are described in the categories of divine creativity, it shows that this event is supposed to correspond to creation in the beginning (Rom. 4.17; 2 Cor. 4.6). In so far as the quickening and resurrection have as their premise the self-surrender, suffering and death of Christ in our stead and for our sakes, they complete the weariness and labour of the Creator in history. Because God in Christ has suffered our closedness (that is to say our death), through Christ's resurrection he opens for us the fullness of his eternal life. Eternal life is no longer a life which is merely preserved from death; it is life that has overcome death altogether. Consequently we have to understand this opening up of eternal life through Christ's death and resurrection as the consummation of the creation process. According to Paul, the crucified Christ has been raised to be the Kyrios, and transformed into the 'life-giving Spirit'. Consequently the quickening powers of the Spirit proceed from him. In the Pauline doctrine of the charismata, the Spirit is the power of the new creation, as well as the power of the resurrection. And in and through the community of Christ's people, the powers of the new creation are to descend on 'all flesh', so as to quicken it for eternal life.

If we want to interpret salvation in this perspective, we shall have to see it as the ultimate and, in trend, universal opening for the fullness of the divine life of closed and isolated men and women and the closedness of 'this world'. God's openness for the world is manifested in Christ's suffering and death. That is why

Christ's resurrection brings about, in faith, the unshakable openness for God on the part of men and women. 'The revelation of
the Spirit' in the charismata of the community of Christ's people
makes this mutual opening of God and human beings specific in
the opening of the frontiers which men and women set up in
order to cut themselves off from other people: Jews and Gentiles,
Greeks and barbarians, masters and servants, men and women
(Gal. 3.28). Through the charismatic quickening of the world,
the freedom created through Christ's passion and glorification
works as liberation. Wherever possible, openness to God, openness to our neighbour and openness towards nature are forged,
and community in freedom is conferred.

5. The Consummation of Creation

Statements about the future of creation and history in the
kingdom of glory can only be made along the guidelines of
historical remembrance and hope. Ideas which we form in the
midst of history about its end have the form of beginnings. In the
prophetic and apocalyptic visions we find two formal principles:
first, the negation of the negative, and second, the fulfilment of
anticipations. In this double form the visions remain simultaneously realistic and futuristic. The negation of the negative –
'death shall be no more, neither shall there be mourning nor cry-
ing nor pain any more' (Rev. 21.4) – defines the space that is
open for the positive reality that is to come. The vision of 'the
classless society' also follows this method of describing the future
by means of a negation of the negative. But the mere negation of
the negative does not lead to a definition of the positive.
Consequently eschatology too cannot be developed merely as
negative theology.[20] The negation of the negative must itself have
its foundation in the beginnings of the positive, however hidden
these beginnings may be. If this were not the case, what is negative could not be experienced as negative and judged accordingly. For biblical eschatology, the negation of the negative is rooted
in the experiences of the divine promissory history, which let us

seek after fulfilment. The two patterns, promise-fulfilment and negation-of-the-negative, together mould the pattern of the eschatological visions.

The consummation of the creative process in the kingdom of glory is conceived and presented as *God's indwelling* in the new creation. 'Behold, the dwelling of God is with men. He will dwell with them, and they shall be his people' (Rev. 21.3). It is no longer merely heaven that is named as the place where God dwells; heaven and earth are now to be newly created so that God himself may dwell in them: *finitum capax infiniti* – the finite is able to contain the infinite. In the consummation, the hidden, historical indwellings of God in temple and people are to be universally fulfilled. At the creation in the beginning there was as yet no talk of such an indwelling. But creation was to be open for it, and aligned towards it. 1 Corinthians 15 links this fulfilment of creation and promissory history with the negation of the negative: '[He will destroy] every rule and every authority and power . . . The last enemy to be destroyed is death' (vv. 24–26). The Son is to fulfil his liberating rule by giving over the kingdom to the Father 'so that God may be all in all' (v. 28). According to Paul too, the Creator will no longer continue to confront his creation; he will enter into it with his glory, thus permeating everything. This all-permeating presence comprehends the destruction of all destructive forces, and therefore the new creation of all things out of the divine glory. Human beings will not merely be restored as the image of God; they will be 'glorified' (Rom. 3.23; 8.30) – that is to say, given a part in the life and glory of God. Together with human beings, the whole creation will be free from the enslavement of futility and will participate in God's all-permeating glory in its own way. Glorified human beings and glorified creation are consequently finite but no longer mortal; temporal but no longer transitory. The patristic doctrine of *theosis* (deification) tried to think this through against the background of the life of the risen and transfigured Christ.

If we understand finitude as a qualitative term and not a quantitative one (as we must do, if infinity is to be anything other than endlessness) – if we perceive time from change and not merely from transience, so that a change from 'glory into glory' becomes conceivable, then these ideas do not seem so unthinkable.

We have now termed creation at the beginning an open system, and have understood the history of God as being the opening up of closed systems in time. This brings us up against a further question: Do we have to conceive the completion of the process of creation as the final end of the open and opened systems? Is the kingdom of glory the universal system which has finally come to a close? In that case the new creation would be the end of time, and in itself timeless. The open system 'human being' would then be only an unfinished system, and the open systems of nature would be merely systems that are not yet closed. History would be the condition of a cosmos that was not yet completely and thoroughly determined. And the consummation would then be the end of human liberty and the end too of God's potentialities. Time would be ended and gathered up in eternity, and possibility in reality.

But theologically, the consummation cannot be thought of in this way. If the process of creation is to be completed through God's indwelling, then the unlimited fullness of divine potentiality indwells the new creation; and through their participation in the unbounded liberty of God, glorified human beings are unboundedly free. So the indwelling of the limitless fullness of God's potentialities means the openness *par excellence* of all systems of life, and that they will therefore be eternally living systems and not fossilized ones. It will therefore be permissible for us to assume that in the kingdom of glory too there will be time and history, future and possibility – and that they will be given in unimpeded measure and in a way that is no longer ambivalent. Instead of timeless eternity, we would therefore do better to talk about 'eternal time' (*aeon, aevum*), and instead of 'the end of history' to speak of the end of pre-history and the beginning of the 'eternal history' of God, human beings and nature. We must then, certainly, think of change without transience, time without the past, and life without death. And it is difficult to do this in the history of life and death, becoming and passing away, because all our concepts are moulded by these experiences.

Nevertheless, both the structure of the natural system and human experience of history point in this direction. The material structures already show a margin of undetermined behaviour. When we pass from atomic structures to more complex systems, we discover a greater openness to time and a growing wealth of potentiality. With the evolution of more complex systems the indefinability of behaviour grows, because the possibilities increase. Human beings and their social systems are the most complex systems that we know. They show the highest degree of indeterminate behaviour and the widest measure of openness to time and the future. Every realization of potentiality through open systems creates openness for new potentiality; it is by no means the case that potentiality is merely realized, and that the future is transformed into the past. This means that it is impossible to imagine the kingdom of glory, which perfects the process of creation through the indwelling of God, as a system that has finally been brought to a close – that is to say, a closed system. We are bound to conceive of it as the openness of all finite life-systems for God's infinity. This of course also means that the Being of God must no longer be thought of as the highest reality for all realized potentialities, but as the transcendent making-possible of all possible realities.

6. Sustainable Symbioses between Human Beings and Nature

The misunderstanding of creation as a primal, finished and in-itself-perfect condition led traditionally to the view that the true and essential human destiny was to be found in the injunction in Gen. 1.28 'Be fruitful and multiply, and fill the earth and subdue it.' People did not read this injunction in the Priestly Writing in the light of the history of tradition, seeing it in the context of earlier texts, such as the Yahwist (who interpreted this 'having dominion' as 'tilling and keeping'), or in the light of later Old and New Testament passages. Instead they related all the later texts to this single 'creation text'. The result was a one-sided stress on the human being's special position in the cosmos. The human being is the thinking subject who rules; all other creatures are subjected to him and are his objects. Human rule over the world was understood as proof that the human being was made in the image of God. Francis Bacon, understanding redemption from the Fall as being the restoration of creation as it originally was, declared that the goal of the scientific elucidation of nature was 'the restitution and reinvesting (in great part) of man to the sovereignty and power . . . which he had in his first state of creation'. The restoration of human sovereignty over the world through science and technology was to make the human being once again God's image on earth. In Bacon and Descartes we can see the fateful reversal of biblical thinking which, with booming technology, has led to today's world-wide ecological crisis. According to the Bible, human beings' creation as image of God is the ground for their rule over the world. According to Bacon and Descartes, the rule of human beings over the world is the ground of their divinity.[21]

Bacon and Descartes described the relationship between human beings and the world as the relation between a subject and an object, and with the general acceptance of this pattern the triumphal progress of classical science and modern technology began. It is a pattern of domination and exploitation. Quantum physics has not, indeed, entirely surmounted this pattern, but it has relativized it: 'The old division of the world into objective processes in space and time and the mind in which these processes are mirrored – in other words, the Cartesian difference between *res cogitans* and *res extensa* – is no longer a suitable starting point for our understanding of modern science. Science, we find, is now focussed on the network of relationships between man and nature, on the framework which makes us as living beings dependent parts of nature, and which we as human beings have simultaneously made the object of our thoughts and actions. Science no longer confronts nature as an objective observer, but sees itself as an actor in this interplay between man and nature.'[22]

It is precisely this reciprocal play which is not comprehended in the pattern of rule and subjection. So we have to develop a new model. According to the pattern of communication and co-operation, nature is no longer the subjugated object of human beings; it is a cohesion of open life-systems with its own subjectivity. Scientifically speaking, the Cartesian phase, in which nature was objectified, has been fundamentally exhausted, and offers no new insights. The recognition of complex open systems in the environment requires a model based on a theory of communication. Two subjects with, of course, a different subjectivity enter into a mutual relationship with each other. Wherever we come across undetermined behaviour in natural systems, we can talk about a certain subjectivity or 'freedom of choice'. The more science advances towards a recognition of more complex systems, the more it will cease to provide merely technically serviceable results, but will also offer findings showing that, out of consideration for our partner 'environment', we must not do what we would be able to do. Investigations into the ecology of survival on the sub-human level have shown that in 'the struggle for existence' symbioses between competing organisms have a far greater chance of survival than conflicts between competing organisms. The subject-object relationship of human beings to nature, and the pattern of domination and exploitation, do not lead to any symbiosis between human and non-human systems that would be capable of survival; they lead to the silencing of nature, and to the ecological death of human beings and nature both.

Because, now, all the processes which change our natural environment have their roots in economic and social processes in human societies, and because these in their turn are based on the human being's interpretation of what he is, it would seem to be a task for Christian theology to push for the revaluation of values that have hitherto been accepted. Human beings will not again become God's image here on earth by subjecting nature to themselves, demolishing the natural systems and exploiting them for their own purposes.

For Christian faith, *Christ* is the 'true human being' and 'the image of God' on earth. That is why 'all authority in heaven and on earth' has been given him (Matt. 28.18). But Christ came 'not to be served' – not to rule – 'but to serve'. And he served in order to make us free for fellowship with God and for openness for one another. In the light of Christ's mission, Gen. 1.28 will have to be interpreted in an entirely new way: not 'subdue the earth' but 'free the earth through community with it'. For according to Romans 8, the whole enslaved creation waits for the revelation of 'the glorious liberty of the children of God', so that it itself may thereby be free. Karl Marx called this 'the true resurrection of nature' and hoped for its emergence from 'a naturalization of the human being' and from the 'humanization of nature'.[23]

For the ethos of human society, the conclusion to be drawn from this is that we need a new orientation, away from the will to power towards solidarity, away from the struggle for existence towards peace in existence, and away from the pursuit of happiness towards community and fellowship. The most important element in the further development of civilization is *social justice*, not the growth of economic power. But we shall not be able to achieve social justice without justice for the natural environment, and we shall not be able to achieve justice for nature without social justice. For the pattern of exploitation has dominated both human labour and nature's resources. If today the 'limits of growth' are becoming evident, and if we are entering a situation where there is going to be a general shortage of foodstuffs, 'doing without' will be unavoidable. Solidarity and community are the values which make unavoidable suffering and necessary sacrifices endurable.

Justice is the form of authentic interdependence between people, and between society and the environment. It is forged in the symbioses between different systems of life, and is the basis for their common survival. Its presupposition is the recognition of the independence and subjectivity of the other life-system. 'Independence, in the sense of liberation from oppression of others, is a requirement of justice. But independence in the sense of isolation from the human community is neither possible nor just. We – human persons – need each other within communities. We – human communities – need each other within the community of mankind. We – mankind – need nature within the community of creation. We – the creation – need God, our Creator and Recreator. Mankind faces the urgent task of devising social mechanisms and political structures that encourage genuine interdependence, in order to replace mechanisms and structures that sustain domination and subservience.'[24]

The outline of an eschatological doctrine of creation with the help of a theory of open systems and their communication, should serve this task. For if the task is not fulfilled, human beings and nature have no chance of survival.

7. What Will Be 'New' in the New Creation of All Things?

In her excellent book *Creation through Wisdom*,[25] Celia Deane-Drummond several times maintains that in my theology the relation between creation and new creation remains unexplained. Indeed she calls it an 'enigma in Moltmann's theology'. This uncertainty is remarkable, for she wrote her Manchester dissertation on *Ecology in Jürgen Moltmann's Theology* (1977). Or have I really hitherto expressed myself so confusingly and obscurely? At all events, let me try here in a few sentences to express myself as clearly as possible, so as to solve the enigma.

 1. Every consciously Christian idea about the eschatological new creation of all things will take its bearings from the raising of the crucified Christ. Eschatological questions receive a christological answer first of all, because this can be given with certainty. It is not another Christ who has taken the place of the dead Jesus. It is the same Jesus who appeared to the disciples, women and men, in the radiance of God's glory and identified himself through the marks of the nails as the one crucified. It is the crucified body which through the raising became the 'glorified body' (Phil. 3.21). God raised the crucified Jesus from the 'form of a servant' to his divine form (Phil. 2.5–11). So in him and with him the eschatological new creation of all things has already begun.

 2. Through faith, a community with Christ comes into being

which is so close that human beings live 'in Christ' and 'Christ in them'. This means the risen and present Christ. 'If anyone is in Christ, he is a new creation, the old has passed away, behold all things have become new' (2 Cor. 5.17). So the new creation of human existence begins in community with the risen Christ. In the fellowship of Christ the Holy Spirit is experienced as the Spirit of new life. Men and women are 'born again' from God's Spirit (John 3.3). What is meant by this is the rebirth to the eternal life of the future world. So these people experience the energies of the divine Spirit as 'the powers of the world to come' (Heb. 6.5).

3. The eschatological new creation of all things takes in human beings in that End-time transformation process (1 Cor. 15.52), in which according to Paul 'the corruptible' becomes incorruptible and 'the mortal' immortal, because death 'is destroyed' (15.26) and 'is swallowed up' (15.54) in the victory of life. The 'eschatological moment' in which this takes place has to be understood not just synchronically but *diachronically* too. It reaches the living and the dead, from the first human being to the last. The identity of created beings is preserved, but the form their lives take (the form of mortality) is transformed into the form of life which is immortality. According to Rev. 21.5, God promises: 'Behold, I make all things new.' What is promised is not another, new creation. It is the new creation of everything that has already been created. What is to be expected cannot be another world; it must be the fundamental alteration of the existing one. This emerges, first, from the premised 'all', and second, from the divine 'make', which in Hebrew, as *asa*, form, shape, is to be distinguished from create, *bara*, which means to call out of non-existence into existence.

4. If these are the essential data in Christian eschatology for the vision of the new creation, then we can sum up systematically what is to become 'new':

(a) It will be a universal and final *transformation process* – not a continuation of world history, and not an annihilation of the world's existence either, but the conferral of a new form to its being-as-it-is.

(b) The temporal creation in the beginning – it was created

'with time' (*cum tempore*), as Augustine said – will become the *eternal* creation. It is not only death that will be overcome but the very possibility of death. Mortal living things will become *immortal* living things. It is not only sin that will be overcome but the very possibility of sin. A creation threatened by evil and annihilation will become a creation in which God 'is all in all' (1 Cor. 15.28) and which is therefore *indestructible*.

(c) The ground and origin of this transformation in the foundations of creation is to be found in the *new relationship to God*. The Creator does not merely stand over against his creation. He enters into it as well, without being absorbed into it. If he was already present in his creation from the beginning through his Wisdom and his Spirit – if he already indwelt Israel through his Name and his Shekinah – if the eternal Logos became 'flesh' in Jesus Christ (John 1.1–3) – if the eternal Spirit indwells believers – if all this is so, then his eschatological presence in the world has to be viewed as *the universal indwelling of his glory* (Isa. 6.3). Here are fulfilled the promise given to the nations with the particular indwelling of God in Israel (Rev. 21.3), and the promises given with the incarnation of Christ and the outpouring of the Spirit 'on all flesh', so that we can talk about the *cosmic* Shekinah, and the *cosmic* incarnation, and the *cosmic* interpenetration with the Spirit and transfiguration of the world.

(d) If from this future we look back to creation in the beginning, we perceive that all created beings are *true promises* of this, their own future in the kingdom of God, and we see in what way. They all point beyond themselves into this future. If we look at the history of the creation, then God's preservation of creation is directed towards this, its new creation. In his providence his promise is concealed. In my view, natural theology is an essential task for Christian theology. It is an anticipation of the eschatological theology of glory in and for nature.

I should not like to claim that this makes everything clear, but I hope that with what I have said I have made my own ideas about the new creation of things sufficiently clear.

IV

God's Self-Restriction and the History of the Universe

As a theologian, I should like to begin this chapter with an account of Christian and Jewish kenotic theology. I shall then go on to ask about its possible relevance for an understanding of God's presence and activity in the universe. A theological doctrine of creation is not a religious cosmology which enters the lists in competition with the cosmologies of physics. But it has to be compatible with physical cosmologies.[1]

The theological account of experiences of God is different from the scientific account of experiences of nature. If we bring them into dialogue with each other, two things soon emerge. First, theologians have a predilection for the 'great scientific narratives', with their unique and unrepeatable histories, because these narratives correspond to God's histories. One of these narratives is the development of the expanding cosmos since the 'Big Bang'; the other is the evolution of life in 'the phylogenetic tree'. Second, theologians have a particular interest in a natural phenomenon for which scientists have no great liking: 'contingency'. We know from the unpredictable chances in human life and in our own personal biographies that these chances can put paid to our plans, for both good and ill. Sociologists such as Jürgen Habermas and Hermann Lübbe therefore see the very function of religion as being 'the mastery of contingency': So in developing a theology of nature, we have to ask about God's presence in the history of nature and in the chance events that herald a future which cannot be extrapolated from the past and present of the cosmos. We shall see whether here Christian and Jewish kenotic theology can sharpen our insight.

1. The Christian Theology of Christ's Kenosis

Christian experience of God springs from the perception of the presence of God in Jesus Christ and his history. According to the hymn which Paul quotes in Phil. 2.5–11, Christ's history was understood as a *kenosis* – a self-emptying – for the sake of the redemption of God-forsaken men and women:

> Have this mind among yourselves, which is also in Christ
> Jesus;
> who, though he was in the form of God,
> did not count equality with God a thing to be grasped,
> but emptied himself, taking the form of a servant,
> being born like another. And being found in human form
> he humbled himself and became obedient unto death,
> even death on the cross. Therefore God has highly exalted
> him . . .

The history of Christ which the first part of this hymn describes begins with the 'divine form' of the Son of God in heaven and ends with the 'form of a servant' on the cross at Golgotha. The becoming-human of Christ presupposes the 'self-emptying' of his divine form and the 'humbling of himself' that follows – his self-humiliation. God's eternal Son becomes human and mortal. He becomes the servant of human beings and dies on the cross. He does all this out of 'obedience' to God the Father. I shall not go here into the many individual exegetical problems,[2] but shall turn directly to the theological ones.

1. Early Lutheran theology tried to understand this *kenosis* or self-emptying of the Son of God in the light of the christological doctrine of Christ's two natures.[3] Christ's *kenosis* means that in becoming human Christ renounces the attributes of divine majesty, so that he is not almighty, omnipresent and omniscient, but becomes 'like another human being' – that is to say, a limited

being, who encounters other human beings in human way. But it was only in respect of his human nature that he 'renounced' the divine attributes (as the Giessen theologians said) or 'concealed' them (as the seventeenth-century Tübingen theologians explained). Neither group was prepared to talk about a *kenosis* of the *divinity* of the eternal Logos. They merely wished to make room for the true and real humanity of Christ's life on earth.

In the nineteenth century, the Lutheran 'kenotics' (Sartorius, Liebner, Hofmann, Thomasius, Frank and Gess) initiated a new approach. Following patristic theology, they assumed that the subject of the *kenosis* described in Philippians 2 was not the Christ-who-has-become-human, but the Christ-in-his-becoming-human. His *kenosis* does not relate only to the attributes of majesty inherent in his divine nature; it already touches the divine being of the eternal Logos itself. The Son of God-human being, taught Thomasius, proceeds out of 'a self-limitation of the divine'. Christ's human form, which is the form of a servant, therefore takes the place of his original divine form. But if in the incarnate Son of God other human beings do not encounter anything divine, how could they then recognize him as the Christ of God at all? To this objection the kenotics replied – although admittedly with some degree of embarrassment – by postulating a dichotomy in the divine attributes: the incarnate Son of God 'renounces' the divine attributes of majesty as these are related to the world, but retains the inner attributes which constitute God's essential nature: truth, holiness, love. For the act of *kenosis* is an act of God's free love for men and women.

To split the attributes of the Godhead in this way, as presupposition for the incarnation and the *kenosis* of the Son of God, remained so unsatisfactory that the nineteenth-century Lutheran kenotics found no successors. But they had detected a real problem for all that. The attributes of deity which are related to the world (omnipotence, omnipresence, omniscience, immortality, impassibility and immutability) derive from Aristotle's general metaphysics. They have very little to do with God's attributes according to the history of God to which the Bible testifies. So they cannot, either, be the attributes of the God in whom people believe 'for Christ's sake', and whom they therefore call 'the Father of Jesus Christ'. For that God 'is in Christ' according to Paul (2 Cor. 5.19), 'dwells in Christ' according to the Gospel of John (14.11), and is known and worshipped *in* the Son.

This brings us to the other attempt at understanding Christ's *kenosis*.

2. Instead of interpreting the *kenosis* in the framework of the christological doctrine of the two natures, Hans Urs von Balthasar sees it in the context of the doctrine of the Trinity.[4] It is the essential nature of the eternal Son of the eternal Father to be 'obedient' in complete love and self-surrender, just as it is the essential nature of the eternal Father to communicate himself in complete love to the Son. If the incarnate Son becomes 'obedient' to the will of the eternal Father to the point of death on the cross, then what he does on earth is no different from what he does in heaven, and what he does in time is no different from what he does in eternity. So in 'the form of a servant' he does not deny his divine form, nor does he conceal it or renounce it; he reveals it. In his obedience he realizes on earth his eternal relationship to the Father. By virtue of the love for the Father which is intrinsic to his nature, he is in his obedience to the point of death on the cross wholly one with the Father. For it is not just that he 'empties' himself 'to' the human being, and in the human being 'to' the being of a servant, and in human mortality 'to' the cruel death on the cross; in all these things he empties himself in obedience to the will of his divine Father in heaven. So *kenosis* is not a self-limitation and self-renunciation on God's part; it is the self-realization in time of the eternal self-surrender of the Son to the Father in the trinitarian life of God. By virtue of limitless love, the inner life of the Trinity takes its impress from the reciprocal 'primordial *kenosis*' of the divine Persons in relation to one another. The Son by virtue of his self-surrender exists wholly in the Father, the Father wholly in the Son, the Spirit wholly in the Father and the Son. Kenotic self-surrender is God's trinitarian nature, and is therefore also the mark of all his works 'outwards': the creation, reconciliation and redemption of all things.

This attempt to explain the *kenosis* of Christ according to Philippians 2 by drawing on trinitarian doctrine goes beyond the interpretations of the nineteenth-century kenotics, and is the next logical step. But it completely dispenses with the attributes of God which are related to the world and are understood metaphysically, and draws solely on the mutual inner-trinitarian relations of the Son to the Father and – as they are seen in the second part of the hymn – of the Father to the Son. This presupposes that the world of human beings and death does not exist outside God, but that from the very beginning it belongs within the mystery of the Trinity: the Father created the world out of love for the Son – the Son redeems the world out of love for the Father. If, conversely, we wanted to see the world outside the triune God, we should have to conjoin these inner-trinitarian relationships with God's relationships to the world; and then either go back, after all, to talking about the metaphysical attributes (omnipotence, immutability, and the rest) or, alternatively, would have to reformulate these world-related divine attributes in a new sense – that is to say biblically and christologically.

We have the kenotics to thank for at last having made the contradiction plain: the God who is metaphysically described in negative terms cannot suffer and cannot change; the God of the biblical history, in contrast, is 'faithful', but he can also 'repent' – 'be sorry'; he is full of passion and compassion; and for that reason he is able to love and to suffer.[5]

We shall come back at the end to the new formulation of God's attributes in relation to the world which then becomes necessary, and I shall offer some suggestions.

2. The Jewish Theology of God's Shekinah

In the idea of the Shekinah – God's 'indwelling' – we find the Old Testament presupposition for the Christian idea of Christ's *kenosis*, and its Jewish equivalent.[6]

God's promise: 'I will dwell in the midst of the Israelites' is already implicit in the covenant made with the chosen people: 'I will be your God and you shall be my people.'[7] The eternal, infinite God whom even the heavens cannot contain 'comes down' (Ex. 3.8), so as 'to dwell' among his powerless little people. Israel's history tells about this indwelling of God in vivid and pictorial terms. God led his people out of slavery in Egypt into the liberty of the promised land, and went ahead of them in 'the pillar of cloud by day' and 'the pillar of fire' by night. He dwelt on the Ark of the covenant (the transportable altar of God's wandering people) until David brought the Ark to Mount Zion, where King Solomon then built the Temple for it. In the Holy of Holies of the Temple, the 'indwelling' of God among the Israelites was present.

But what happened to the Shekinah when in 587 BC the Babylonians destroyed city and Temple? Did God withdraw his earthly 'indwelling' to his eternal presence in heaven? That would have been the end of his covenant, and the death of Israel as God's people. Or did his Shekinah go into Babylonian exile with the captured people, remaining 'in the midst of the Israelites', even though it was now itself homeless, humiliated, exiled, and exposed to the persecutions of the powerful nations and their gods? This second answer has kept Israel's faith in God alive in destruction and exile down to the present day. Ever since, God's Shekinah has been the comrade on the way and the companion in suffering of the homeless Israelites. The people suffer persecution and exile, and God's indwelling suffers with them. 'In all their afflictions he was afflicted' (Isa. 63.9). Out of these Israelite experiences of the shared suffering of God's Shekinah rabbinic literature later conceived the theology of God's self-humiliation.[8] This theology led to the hope that at the end, with the redemption of the people from their suffering, God's Shekinah itself will be redeemed from the suffering it shares with the people, and with them will return to its eternal home.

This brings us to the theological interpretations of Israel's experiences of the Shekinah.

1. In his theology of Israel's prophets, *Abraham Heschel* developed from Israel's experience of the Shekinah and its Sh'ma

prayer to the one God a 'bipolar concept' of that One God. In history, God exists in a twofold presence: in heaven, and in his exiled people – unlimited and limited – infinite and finite – free from suffering and death, while at the same time suffering and dying together with his people.[9]

2. *Franz Rosenzweig*, drawing on Hegel's dialectic, interpreted Israel's experience of the Shekinah as a 'self-differentiation in God': 'God himself cuts himself off from himself, he gives himself away to his people, he suffers with their sufferings, he goes with them into the misery of the foreign land, he wanders with their wanderings.'[10] He talked about a 'divine suffering' on the part of 'the banished God', who in fellowship with his people makes himself 'in need of redemption'. This 'redemption of God' is the homecoming of the once separated Shekinah to the fullness of the One God. Something of this takes place in every Sh'ma Israel prayer, for in the acknowledgement of the One God, God himself is 'united', according to Rosenzweig. God will be finally redeemed and united when the One God becomes the All-One God and is 'all in all', as he says with 1 Cor. 15.28. Then heaven and earth will become God's dwelling place and all created being will participate in God's indwelling livingness and glory.

3. Is the Creation of the World Linked with an Act of Kenosis on God's Part?

In the next two sections we shall turn to the creation of the world and the history of creation, asking about the possible significance of the *kenosis* idea for the presence of God and his future in creation and in the preservation of the world.

In our hymns we find two verses in which the Creator and sustainer of the world is conceived of in 'the form of a servant' which Christ assumes.

In a Christmas hymn, Luther writes of the God who 'lays aside his might' and assumes the form of weakness:[11]

> Er äussert sich all seiner G'walt,
> wird niedrig und gering,

> und nimmt an sich ein's Knechts Gestalt,
> der Schöpfer aller Ding.

And W. H. Vanstone:

> Thou art God, no monarch Thou
> thron'd in easy state to reign.
> Thou art God, whose arms of love
> aching, spent, the world sustain.[12]

In his Christmas hymn Luther sees in 'the self-emptying Christ' the Creator of the world, while Vanstone sees in the sustainer of the world 'the crucified God'. With these figures of speech, both writers express the conviction that the creation and sustaining of the world are not simply works of the almighty God, but that in them God gives himself and communicates himself, and is thus himself present in his works.

(a) Is creation an act of *divine self-definition?* If in his freedom God resolves to create a being who is not divine, but who can co-exist with his own divine being, then this resolve does not affect the created being only; it touches God's own being too. He determines himself to be the Creator who lets a creation co-exist with himself.[13] Logically speaking, God's self-determination to be the Creator precedes the act of creation. God determines himself before he determines the world. It is therefore correct to see God's self-determination to be the Creator of a non-divine world as already a *self-limitation* on God's part: (1) out of his infinite possibilities God realizes this particular one, and renounces all the others; (2) God's determination to be Creator is linked with the *consideration for his creation* which allows it space and time and its own movement, so that it is not crushed by the divine reality and totally drawn or absorbed into its infinitude. By differentiating himself as Creator from a created world, God creates a reality which is not divine but is not Nothing either, and preserves that reality by distancing himself from it.

How can a finite world co-exist with the infinite God? Does it set a limit to the limitless God, or does God limit himself? If this limit or frontier between infinity and finitude is already 'fore-given' to God, then God is not infinite. If God is in his very essence infinite, then any such limit or frontier exists only through his *self-limitation*. That makes it possible for a finite world to co-exist with God. This self-limitation of God's which is given with the differentiation between Creator and creation is viewed in theology as the first act of grace. For the limitation of his infinity and omnipresence is itself an act of his own omnipotence. Only God can limit God.

(b) Is creation an act of *divine self-contraction?* Before God went out of himself in order to create a non-divine world, he withdrew into himself in order to make room for the world, and to concede it a space. That was Isaac Luria's idea. He called it *zimzum*. According to the Kabbalah, the infinite Holy One, the One whose light primordially filled the whole universe, withdrew his light and concentrated it wholly on his own substance, thereby creating empty space.[14] God withdrew his omnipresence in order to concede space for the limited presence of the creation. In this way creation comes into being in the space of God's *kenosis*. In the dispute between Newton, with his idea about absolute space, and Leibniz, with his notion of relative spaces, Henry More introduced this Jewish-kabbalistic idea of *makom-kadosh* into the discussion, though without perceiving the possibilities it offered for solving this dispute about the concept of space.[15] Gershom Scholem used Luria's *zimzum* idea to provide new explanatory grounds for the Jewish-Christian concept of the *creatio ex nihilo*, the creation out of nothing: 'Where God withdraws himself from himself to himself, he can call something forth which is not of divine essence or divine being.'[16] Speaking metaphorically, when God contracts himself in order creatively to go out of himself, then in his self-contraction he gathers together his creative energies. It may be noted in passing that in interpreting the 'Big Bang' (*Urknall*), scientifically similar metaphors are used to explain the primal impetus (*Urschwung*) out of which the expanding universe came into being.

(c) Is creation an act of *divine self-humiliation?* Many Christian theologians from Nicholas of Cusa down to Emil Brunner have seen God's commitment to this finite and fragile creation as a first act of self-humiliation on God's part, an act which found its continuation in his descent to his people of Israel and reached its profoundest point in Christ's self-surrender to death on the cross.[17] 'The Lamb slain from the foundation of the world' (Rev. 13.8) is a symbol showing that there was already a cross in the heart of God before the world was created and before Christ was crucified on Golgotha. From the creation, by way of reconciliation, right down to the redemption, God's self-humiliations and self-emptyings deepen and unfold. Why? Because the creation proceeds from God's love, and this love respects the own, personal existence of all things, and the freedom of the human beings who have been created. A love which gives the beloved space, allows them time, and asks and expects of them freedom is the power of lovers who can withdraw in order to allow the beloved to grow and to come. Consequently it is not just self-giving which belongs to creative love; it is self-limitation too; not only affection, but respect for the unique nature of the other as well. If we apply this perception to the Creator's relation to his created beings, what follows is a *restriction* of God's omnipotence, omnipresence and omniscience, so that those he has created may have room to live.

Hans Jonas took up the *zimzum* idea early on, linking it first with the evolutionary world picture, and later also with experiences of death in Auschwitz.[18] For him, 'omnipotence' is a meaningless concept, because almighty power is power without an object, and would therefore be a powerless power. 'Power is a relational term', and links a dominating subject with a dominated object. God's creative power therefore admits or embraces a 'self-renunciation of unlimited power' for the sake of created beings. If God as Creator commits himself to this world, he at the same time delivers himself up to this 'world-in-its-becoming'. Whatever happens to it, happens to God too. As Creator, God becomes part of the fate of the world. Hans Jonas calls this fate 'the odyssey of the universe'. God becomes dependent on the world, as the world is dependent on him. They share a common history.

Kierkegaard detected similar lines of thought in Hegel's idea of world history as 'God's biography', and maintained in opposition that only almighty power can limit itself, can give itself and withdraw itself, in order to make the recipient independent; so that in the divine act of self-humiliation we also have to respect an act of God's omnipotence.[19] We might put it epigrammatically and say that God never appears mightier than in the act of his self-limitation, and never greater than in the act of his self-humiliation.

What can be said about the self-limitation of omnipotence in God's love for those he has created can be said about the other metaphysical attributes of his divinity too: omnipresence, omniscience, invulnerability, and self-sufficiency. God doesn't know everything in advance because he doesn't will to know everything in advance. He waits for the response of those he has created, and lets their future come. God is not incapable of suffering; he opens himself in his Shekinah for the sufferings of his people, and in the incarnation of the Son for the sufferings of the love which desires to redeem the world. So in a certain way God becomes dependent on the response of his beloved creatures. In Christian theology one would not go so far as to declare God 'in need of redemption' together with his people Israel; but nevertheless, God has laid the sanctification of his Name and the doing of his will in the hands of human beings, and thus also, in its own way, the coming of his kingdom. It must be viewed as part of God's self-humiliation that God does not desire to be without those he has created and loves, and therefore waits for them to repent and turn back, leaving them time, so that he may come to his kingdom together with them.

4. The Preservation and Consummation of Creation through God's Patience and the Driving Energies of His Spirit

If the creation of a world not divine is already linked with a kenotic self-limitation on God's part, how much more can this then be said about its preservation for its consummation. In his relation to the world, God is not almighty in the sense that as

First Cause (*causa prima*) he effects everything in everything through the secondary causes (*causa secundae*) – good and evil, becoming and passing away, genesis and dissolution. The person who assumes that this is the way in which (in the words of the hymn) God 'so wondrously reigneth' ends up with the unanswerable theodicy question: if God is almighty, why evil? Either he is omnipotent and effects everything, in which case he is not good; or he is good, but then he cannot be almighty. But if we start from God's *kenosis*, we discover his almighty power in his almighty suffering patience, as Russian Orthodox theology says. It is not God's power that is almighty. What is almighty is his love, about which Paul says: 'Love is long-suffering and kind . . . It bears *all things*, believes *all things*, hopes *all things*, endures *all things*' (1 Cor. 13. 4, 7). In this eulogy of love, Paul heaps up the words invoking the 'all'. Through the power of his patience God sustains this world with all its contradictions and conflicts. As we know from human history, patience is the most powerful action because it has time, whereas acts of violence never have time and can therefore win only short-term victories. Patience has the upper hand. God does not sustain and rule the world like an autocrat or a dictator, who permits no freedom; he is more like a suffering servant who bears the world with its guilt and its griefs as Atlas carries the world on his shoulders.

To put it without these metaphors: God acts in the history of nature and human beings through his patient and silent presence, through which he gives those he has created space to unfold, time to develop, and power for their own movement. We look in vain for God in the history of nature or in human history if what we are looking for are merely special divine interventions. Is it not much more that God waits and awaits, that – as process theology rightly says – he 'experiences' the history of the world and human beings, that he is 'patient and abounding in steadfast love', as Psalm 103.8 puts it? Israel's psalms never tire of praising God's great goodness and patience. It is because of this steadfast goodness that 'we are not consumed' (Lam. 3.22 AV) – 'not yet wholly cut off', to follow Luther's translation.

But why should God bear and endure the world with its

contradictions and conflicts and catastrophes? According to Aristotelian metaphysics (which have been taken over by Christian theology down to the present day), God is the supreme reality (*summum ens*) and pure act (*actus purus*). All reality is derived from, and is caused by, the highest reality, which is God, and therefore points towards this divine reality. Consequently God must also be the power who is all-efficacious in everything. It was only with Kierkegaard and Heidegger that a new idea began to take shape: 'higher than actuality stands *possibility*.'[20] And all actuality is nothing other than 'realized possibility'. Possibility can become actuality, but actuality can never again become possibility.

If we put these two modalities of being together with the two modes of time, future and past, then future is the sphere of possibilities, but past the realm of actuality. So the future is 'higher' than the past, because in history the future turns into irreversible past, whereas the past never again becomes future. If we switch over from the metaphysics of reality to a metaphysics of possibility, we can then view divine Being as the supreme possibility, as the source of possibilities, and as the transcendental making-possible of the possible. In the theology of time, what corresponds is then the future as the transcendent source of time, as Georg Picht has shown, following Heidegger.[21]

If we apply this to our problem, it means that the God who in patience bears and endures the history of nature and human beings allows them time and gives time, and in so doing makes possible ever-new possibilities, which are either realized or not realized, which can be used for further development but also for annihilation. All systems of matter and life are complex systems with a fixed actuality/past and, in each case, a specifically open future/scope of possibility. Their present is the interface between the two times in which more complex structures of reality can be built up. With them the scope of possibilities also grows in each given case. But possibilities can be realized in a negative sense too, and then these open systems destroy themselves.

It is in the gift of the future and the stream of new possibilities that we have to perceive God's activity in the history of open systems of matter and life – and it is out of these open systems that the world we know exists.[22] This means, not least, that all open systems point beyond themselves to the sphere of what they can be, and must be read theologically as real, or true, symbols of that future in which they are *in* God and God is in them, when they will participate unhindered in God's indwelling fullness of possibility without being destroyed by it, and will become that for which God has destined them. The goal of God's *kenosis* in the creation and preservation of the world is that *future* which we trace out with the symbols of the kingdom of God and the new creation, or 'world without end'.

V

Eschatological Perspectives on the Future of the Universe

The theme of this symposium sponsored by the John Templeton Foundation is 'The Far-Future Universe: Eschatology from a Cosmic Perspective'.[1] But I am not a scientist. I am a Christian theologian. So I am going to turn the subject upside down, and talk about the eschatological perspectives which emerge for the future of the universe from Christian theology.

In its two-thousand-year history, Christian eschatology has always been developed in the context of the world picture of its epoch. Today we are required to set that eschatology critically and self-critically in the context of modern astrophysics. For more than two hundred years, developments in the modern sciences have led to the retreat of theology from the conception of the world as a whole, and to its withdrawal to the questions of personal existence and morality. We have ceased to be able to bring human eschatology and cosmic eschatology into some degree of harmony. Often this harmony is not even desired by either side – on the scientific side because the trial of Galileo is still unforgotten; on the theological side because the scientific hypotheses are involved in a continually accelerating paradigm change, so that it is impossible to know with what one has to engage. Today only a few scientists read theological books, and theologians dispense almost entirely with scientific reading. Neither side expects much from the other. So today theologians confine themselves to the interpretation of the sacred texts of their traditions, and take no interest in what can be seen through the Hubble space telescope. On the other side, the scientific community is so wrapped up in the need for progress (because of the competition in their scientific fields) that its members expend little thought on the hermeneutical premises of their ways of thinking and their concepts, or on what Habermas calls the 'knowledge-constitutive interest' that prompts their investigations at the present time.

I find this state of things unsatisfactory, and would plead for a new 'natural theology', in which scientific findings tell us something about God, and theological insights something about nature.[2] The reason for a natural theology of this kind is that there is a correspondence between human intelligence and the intelligibility of the universe. We perceive and know more about the world than we need in order to survive in our earthly environment.

1. Theological Origins of Eschatological Perspectives on the Future of the Universe

Theology does not acquire its eschatological horizons from the general observation of the world – neither from the observation of the stars in the universe nor from a contemplation of the events of world history; it acquires them from its particular experience of God. We call this 'root experience', because what is experienced here are events in which God 'reveals' himself, and from which human communities acquire their identity.

For Israel and Judaism this root experience is the Exodus, as the First Commandment states: 'I am the Lord your God, who brought you out of the land of Egypt, out of the house of bondage' (Ex. 20.2). In the Passover feast every generation in Judaism identifies itself with the Exodus generation, and through this identification finds assurance of God and of itself.

For Christianity, the root experience is the Christ event, Christ's self-surrender to death on the cross and his resurrection from the dead. In the celebration of the Eucharist, every Christian congregation places itself within Christ's sphere of influence, and there finds its own assurance of God and of itself.

The religious communities of Judaism and Christianity, then, have emerged out of these special historical root experiences. But these experiences also embrace from the outset general horizons of experience, and universal expectations of the future; for they are experiences in time of the eternal God.

The God who frees Israel from enslavement is perceived *in* all things as the Creator of all things. He led the prisoners into freedom through his activity in history, and similarly, through his creative activity he called everything out of non-being into existence, and brought it out of chaos into a wise order. Consequently heaven and earth are not themselves divine. They are neither 'the body of God' nor are they inhabited by fertility deities who have to be worshipped. They are God's creation. They are a 'work of his hands', as the image or metaphor says; but they are blessed and preserved by God. From early on, the Israelite belief in creation desacralized the world and 'stripped it of its magic', as Max Weber put it, and by doing so it also threw the world open for the scientific and technological intervention of human beings. But that does not mean that this belief in creation has surrendered nature to ecological extermination through modern civilization.[3]

The God who brought Christ out of death into the liberty of the new, eternally living creation is perceived not only as the Creator of all things but also as the one who brings all things to completion. He is 'the God . . . who gives life to the dead and calls into existence the things that do not exist' (Rom. 4.17). From the moment when the disciples called that which happened to the dead Christ 'resurrection from the dead', the universal eschatological horizon was already present in the understanding of this unique historical event. Christ's resurrection 'from the dead' was understood, as the phrase shows, as the beginning of the general resurrection of all the dead. He was called 'the first fruits of those who have fallen asleep' and 'the leader of life'.[4] Whatever 'end' the human world or the natural universe may otherwise have, this future of God's has already begun. The new creation already begins in the midst of the old one. In the community of Christ, believers already experience here and now 'the powers of the age to come' (Heb. 6.5). Because the Christ event is an experience of God, Christian eschatology cannot be reduced to human eschatology, and human eschatology cannot be brought down to the salvation of the soul in a heaven beyond. There are no human souls without human bodies, and no human existence without the life system of this earth, and no earth without the universe. Very early on, Christian eschatology as it developed already brought out the cosmic dimensions of the Christ event, as the (post)Pauline epistles to the Ephesians and the Colossians show. Without an eschatology of the universe, Christian eschatology cripples the Godness of its God.

But this brings us up against the first problem of Christian eschatology: can human and cosmic eschatology still be thought together nowadays, and brought into harmony?

2. Human and Cosmic Eschatology

The biblical traditions are dominated by a strong anthropological principle. Both Israel's creation narratives (Genesis 1–3) are aligned towards the creation of human beings, and put that at the centre. But we know today that *homo sapiens* was a late birth in the evolution of life. The biblical traditions knew nothing about the millions of years of dinosaurian history. On the other hand, the images of the future in the eschatology of the Bible all expect that the end of this world will coincide with the end of the human race. 'The kingdom of God' will come 'in this generation', or after the redemption of Israel, or whenever God wills it; but at all events, according to the Christian creed Christ will come 'to judge the quick and the dead' – so he will still find living human beings. Yet we know today that humanity as a whole is mortal, and that 'the far-future universe' could be a universe without human beings – or at least without human beings as we know them now. This means that it is impossible to shift human protology back to the Big Bang, and to extend human eschatology to the death of the universe through heat or cold. This has considerable consequences for the orientation of human beings in the universe: can human eschatology only give us a limited hope for a meaningful life which is surrounded by a meaningless universe? What conclusions do we have to draw from Steve Weinberg's insight: 'The more the universe seems comprehensible, the more it seems pointless'?[5] Do we exist on an island of meaning in an ocean of meaninglessness?

Another image emerges if we supplement the introduction of the *anthropological* principle into the cosmos through the introduction of the *cosmic* principle into anthropology. We then don't only see the universe in the human being, and the human being as the highest complex, self-conscious system known to us. We see the reverse as well: the human being in the universe, and the universe as the widest context for the development of human potentialities. The future of the universe would then not be bound to the future of human beings; instead the future of human beings would be integrated into the future of the universe. Just as there are an inexhaustible number of thoughts and ideas in the human mind, there can similarly be an inexhaustible number of conditions in the universe. Just as the human mind grasps its potentialities according to its constructive hope and its destructive fears, the continual appearance of new possibilities, similarly, can constitute the universe's openness to the future. Is there a correspondence between complexity and consciousness? Why should the human mind only be involved cognitively in the shaping of the universe, and not constructively too?

If we start from these presuppositions, we have to ask what cosmological utopia and what 'knowledge-constitutive interest' prompt us in our desire to know the universe, and to ask about human possibilities of shaping it.[6] Whatever else our richly proliferating scientific fiction tells us: a fundamental utopia is evidently the endless survival of the human race, and the endless further development of the human consciousness. Unconsciously or consciously we want to overcome death and to live as long as possible: longevity. Immortality was once a religious dream. Today organ transplantation, the attachment of the brain to computers, and other developments seem to have brought immortality within our reach.

By computerizing all the available data, we make synchronic for ourselves what in time takes place successively. In so doing we transfer past and future into present simultaneity, and 'spatialize' time. 'The future is now', says the internet advertisement.

Yet at the same time, through space travel, space stations and landings on other planets we seek for ways of escape, for the day when we have made earth 'too hot to hold us' because we have destroyed it.

In the universe we are ultimately seeking for traces of a 'world without end'. Multiverse models, the genesis of new universes, and limitless expansions of these multiverses point to an end-less future; is it really so, or is it only so because that is what we are searching for?

But is an end-less future for life and the universe as we know it really desirable anyway? Aren't death and the transitoriness of time factors of the finite world which is developing itself for continually new possibilities? If death and time were to be overcome, there would no longer ever be anything new. A world without end would be the end of the world.

3. Traditional Ideas about the Future of the Universe

All the ideas about an 'end of the world' presuppose that the world we know here is temporal, not eternal, and therefore has a beginning and an end with time as we now experience it. This means that the universe is involved in a unique movement. Here we call this movement 'history', because it is not clear from the outset that it is a meaningful evolution of the cosmos, a purposeful development, a progression towards new, higher worlds, or the chaotic spread of cosmic devastation.

We can distinguish ideas about the end which have existed in the past and which are held in the present according to whether they talk about a goal (*telos*) or an end (*finis*) of cosmic history.[7] If the history of the universe has a goal, then that is its consummation, and we can talk about a meaningful development, and identify signs of progress, gradual or from one stage to the next.

The last great cosmic system of a finalistic, or purposeful, meta-physics of this kind was conceived by Teilhard de Chardin: in the far-off future of the universe an 'Omega Point' will emerge which will draw the universe and all its parts to itself. This Point does not move towards the universe, but draws the universe to itself through attraction.[8]

But if the history of the universe is to end in a Big Crunch, and if nothing more is to be expected after such a catastrophe, then there is no meaningful development in the history of the universe either, and no purposeful progression, but merely a succession of smaller part-catastrophes in which the final universal catastro-phe is heralded. Not only human history but the history of the universe too is then, as we say, 'just one damned thing after another'.

Theologically, we call ideas about a purposeful progression towards a state of perfection 'millenarian', because they talk about the Golden Age which Virgil foretold, or about a final kingdom of Christ (Revelation 20) in the final stage of history. The concepts of a linear time, with which progress in all the different spheres of life can be measured, and the modern world's faith in progress, are modern secularizations of the old ideas about a millenarian or chiliastic consummation.[9]

We call ideas about a catastrophic rupture of history 'apocalyptic', because Jewish and Christian apocalyptic writings have passed down dreams about the downfall of this world of violence and injustice and death in which people are oppressed. Apocalyptic was not originally the world of metaphysical fairy-tales and their tellers; it was the world of the persecuted and the martyrs. It is 'the religion of the oppressed' (Laternari). In secularized form, we encounter this world of ideas today in exterminism, and in the 'terminator' from outer space whom we meet in science fiction, and who brings about the end.[10]

In Christian eschatology we always find a combination of the two ideas: an end and a beginning, a catastrophe and a new start, farewell and greeting; for eschatology can only be called Christian if it takes its bearings from Israel's Exodus and the Christ event. Israel's bondage and the death of Christ are primal images of catastrophe. The Exodus into the liberty of the promised land, and the resurrection into the eternal life of the future world are primal images of the new beginning. Christ's end on the cross was not the last thing, but became his true beginning in the resurrection and in the Spirit who is the giver of life. The dialectical mystery of Christian eschatology is, to adopt T. S. Eliot's words: 'In my end is my beginning.' That is also what is meant by some words of mine which were quoted in the invitation to this symposium: 'What can a theology of hope tell us about the far-future cosmos that has relevance from a human perspective? Could the "death and raising of the universe" be the "prelude to an unexpected new creation of all things"?' In the light of their experiences of God, Jews and Christians expect a universal Exodus of all things out of their bondage of transience into a 'new heaven and a new earth [where] the former things shall not be remembered or come to mind' (Isa. 65.17); they expect a raising of *all* the dead, and a restoration of all things in a new, eternal creation (Rev. 21.4). It is only then that there will be 'world without end'.

(a) The Annihilation of the World (*annihilatio mundi*)

For a hundred years, from about 1600 to about 1700, Lutheran theology taught that the final destiny of the universe was to be not its transformation but its annihilation: 'The Last Judgement will be followed by the complete end of this world. Except for angels and human beings, everything belonging to this world will be consumed by fire and will dissolve into nothingness. What must be expected therefore is not the world's transformation but a complete cessation of its substance.'[11] Similar notions can be found among modern fundamentalist 'annihilationists'. After the Last Judgement believers will go to heaven but unbelievers will be exterminated, together with the earth. What used to be called hell is now called 'total non-being'.[12]

The theological reason put forward for this view is that angels and believers will be so totally absorbed in the *visio beatifica*, the bliss of contemplating God 'face to face' (1 Cor. 13.12), that they will have no further need of mediations to God by way of this created world. Angels will no longer need the created world of heaven, and human beings will no longer need the created world of earthly things. So heaven and earth, together with the mortal body, will be demolished and destroyed like a scaffolding once God's consummating goal has been reached, that goal being the salvation of souls.

This idea about the eschatological annihilation of the world does not mean just the world in its present form. It means the very substance of creation itself. It means, in fact, a reversal of the creation out of nothing (*creatio ex nihilo*) into a reduction to nothing (*reductio ad nihilum*). Whereas the original creation was a movement out of non-being into being, its end will be the movement out of being into non-being. Adherents of these ideas about the annihilation of the world claim support from certain biblical passages:

2 Peter 3.10: 'But the day of the Lord will come like a thief in the night, and then the heavens will pass away with a loud noise, and the elements will be dissolved with fire, and the earth and the works that are upon it will be burned up ... Wait for and hasten to the coming of the day of God, when the heavens will be kindled and dissolved and the elements will melt with fire'; and then from Rev. 20.11: 'From (God's) presence earth and sky fled away, and no place was found for them' and Rev. 21.1: 'The first heaven and the first earth had passed away ...'

We might see a modern cosmological analogy if, in a future Big Crunch, the universe were perhaps to revert to its condition before the Big Bang.

(b) The Transformation of the World (*transformatio mundi*)

The idea that the world will be annihilated at the end of time is an exception. The general theological expectation of the end is that the universe will be transformed from the state in which we see it now into a condition which is qualitatively new.

The Catholic preface to the Requiem Mass says: '*Vita mutatur non tollitur*' – life will be changed, not destroyed.[13] Aristotle and

Thomas Aquinas defined the soul as *forma corporis,* or the actualization of the body; and according to this definition, death means its transformation, not its extermination. Lutheran theology justified its doctrine of the annihilation of the world on the grounds of God's total freedom with regard to his creation – the One who created it can destroy it too; but Calvinist theology at the same period saw the transcendent foundation of creation in God's faithfulness, and assumed that this was the divine guarantee for the continued existence of the universe. Like mediaeval Catholic theology, it therefore taught the eschatological transformation of the world, not its destruction: 'After Judgement the end of this world will come about, in that God will destroy the world's present condition through fire and . . . out of the old world will make a new world, a new heaven and a new earth imperishable in kind.'[14] The form of the old world was sin, death and transience; the form of the new one will be righteousness and justice, eternal life and imperishability. The eschatological transformation of the universe embraces both the identity of creation and its newness, that is to say both continuity and discontinuity. All the information systems of this world remain in eternity, but transformed.

The biblical data bear out the correctness of this view, over against the doctrine of annihilation, for in both 2 Peter and Revelation the idea of annihilation is followed by hope for 'a new heaven and a new earth in which righteousness dwells' (2 Peter 3.13) and by the vision: 'And I saw a new heaven and a new earth' (Rev. 21.1).

As far as analogies in present-day cosmology are concerned, an eschatological transformation of this kind could be assumed to be a possible completion of the history of the universe, if that history is viewed as a universal information-process with many strata and many ramifications.

(c) The Deification of the World (*deificatio mundi*)

As third theological idea about the end and consummation of the universe we may take the Orthodox eschatology of the 'deification of the cosmos'.[15] Because the word 'transformation' has to do merely with the form of the world but not its relation to God, the Orthodox idea goes a step further: from transformation (*transformatio*) to glorification (*glorificatio*) and deification (*deificatio*). According to Orthodox doctrine, the human person and nature constitute a unity, and are not set over against each other, as they are in the modern western world. So what is promised to the human person applies to the earth and the cosmos too. Human and cosmic eschatology form a unity. There is no human future without the future of the cosmos. Consequently the cosmos will be redeemed when humanity is redeemed, and vice versa. For nature as a whole is destined for God's glory. Just as to be enlightened by the eternal light of God leads to the transfiguration of the human form, so the universe too will be 'deified' when it is transfigured by God's indwelling glory (Isa. 6.3).

The theological foundation for this eschatological perspective on the far-future universe is to be found in the central importance for Orthodox theology of the resurrection of Christ. Through his real and true raising, the body of Christ was 'transfigured' (Phil. 3.21). His raising 'from' the dead is a human and a cosmic event: the risen Christ is the head of the new humanity and the first of all created being, as the Epistle to the Colossians says (1.15). His raising is a resurrection *with* the dead. In the eschatological consummation, God will then appear in glory in his creation, and through his unveiled eternal presence will redeem all things from transience for imperishable participation in his divine life. For the process of creation, the eternal present/ presence of God means simultaneity. All things which in the beginning were created out of nothing, will then be created anew out of God's glory. So in the eternal present/presence of God the eternal creation comes into being. That is what is meant by the 'deification of the cosmos' through a sharing and participation in the eternal life of God. The world does not become God, nor does it dissolve into God's infinitude; it participates as world in God's eternal being. It will become the temple of his eternal presence. That is what is being said with the image of the heavenly Jerusalem, the city of God which comes down to earth: a cosmic temple.

4. The Eschatological Model for the Future of the Universe

The eschatological idea about the future of the universe differentiates its history, in the old apocalyptic way, into two phases, and talks about the time of this world – 'this world-time', and the time of the world to come – 'the future world-time'. These are two qualitatively differentiated aeons. This world-time is the time of the world that is transitory – the future world-time is the time of an abiding and hence eternal world.[16]

This idea also differentiates the given reality of the universe into 'heaven and earth' – 'things visible and invisible', in the words of the Nicene Creed.[17] By this is meant the differentiable strata of being in the one created reality. We can already see this from the fact that the earth, or visible world, is talked about only in the singular, whereas we can speak of 'the heavens' or 'the invisible worlds' in the plural. This gives us an overall picture of an earthly visible universe, and a heavenly, invisible multiverse. The time of the visible universe is *chronos*, the irreversible temporal structure of becoming and passing away. The time of the invisible multiverse is *aeon, aevum*, the reversible temporal structure of cyclical time, for the circle of time counts as the image and reflection of eternity.

Translated into more modern metaphysics, this means that the visible universe consists of reality and potentiality which, seen in terms of time, are related to each other as past and future. The present is the front line – the interface at which potentialities are either realized or not realized. Past reality is fixed, future potentiality is open. Reality is in every case realized potentiality. Potentiality is therefore the mode of being which underlies this world. The world is and will be made out of potentiality. In contrast, the qualitatively different reality of the invisible worlds consists of potencies and potentials (as Schelling puts it) which make visible and earthly potentiality possible without themselves ever being exhausted.[18]

The eternal Being of God is differentiated from the earth and the heavens, the visible and the invisible worlds. Since the worlds are God's creation, the concept of creation designates the qualitative difference between God and the worlds. Over against the irreversible time of the visible world and the reversible time of the invisible worlds, God's time is eternity. Eternity does not mean end-less time, nor does it mean timelessness. It means power over time (*Zeitmächtigkeit*, as German puts it). Seen over against the modes of time of the created worlds, the eternity of the Creator is to be seen in his pre-temporality, his simultaneity and his post-temporality.[19] His eternity surrounds the time of the created worlds from every side, and by doing so confines it to finite time. But in this way his eternity determines itself for irreversible time as the power of future: so there is past future, present future, and future future.[20]

What consequences do these presuppositions have for an understanding of the scientifically explorable universe?

1. The first consequences are negative. The visible universe is not divine, and displays no characteristics that could be called divine. Nor is the visible universe heavenly. It is therefore neither eternal, nor cyclical, nor permanent; it is transitory, temporal, and contingent. The atheism of old, following Feuerbach's method, denied the reality of God in a world beyond, but transferred all God's attributes to this one, to creative human beings and the marvellous universe; and the result was a deification of this world which can only lead to disappointment.

2. The second consequences are positive. This visible universe is certainly temporal, contingent and finite, but it has an eternal, enduring and infinite future in the future new universe. Once the eschatological differentiation into 'this world' and 'the future world' is made, the finitude, contingency and 'pointlessness' of this universe can be accepted. The future new world will bring what we miss in this finite world: the eternal presence of God, and participation in the attributes of this divine presence – that is to say, that which bears its meaning within itself.

That brings us to the question about the transition from 'this world' to 'the future world'. This transition cannot take place like a transition in this world from one stage to another, for then the irreversible time structure which is a mark of our present world would remain. It can only be a matter of a universal transformation of this present world of the kind Rev. 21.4 describes: 'Behold', says God, 'I will make all things new.' This means that everything created, everything that was here, is here, and will be here is to be 'made' new. Whereas 'to create' means calling something into existence, 'to make' means *forming* what has been called into existence already.

The future, new eternal world is therefore to be the new creation of this world we know. When will that happen? That is difficult to answer, because this eschatological moment must simultaneously be the end of irreversible time; so it cannot take place in this time at all.[21] In his great chapter on the resurrection, 1 Corinthians 15, Paul says that this eschatological moment will come about suddenly, 'in the twinkling of an eye, at the last trumpet' (v. 52), and he uses the Platonic word *exaiphnes,* 'on a sudden', for the moment when eternity touches time, ending and gathering it up into itself. 'Then the dead will be raised imperishable . . . and death is swallowed up in victory' (vv. 52, 55).

In that eschatological moment the raising of the dead will take place diachronically, and irreversible time will be reversed and rolled up from its end, as it were, like a scroll. Before the eternity of God which appears in the eschatological moment all times will be simultaneous. The power of transience and the time that cannot be brought back, 'death', will be gathered up into the victory of eternal life. That is the end of the evolution of the living in what we might call the beginning of the re-volution of the dead.

People who have been close to death have sometimes seen their whole lives spread out before their eyes in an instant, as if in a time-lapse film; and in a similar way one could imagine that in the eschatological moment the flash of eternity will light up the universe from its end to its beginning, and make it wholly present.

The eschatological moment will end the linear time which we have here called the irreversible time of this world, and take into itself an element of cyclical time. What will come about is not an eternal return of the same thing, but a *unique* return of everything. The theological concept for this is 'the restoration of all things'[22] in the appearance of God's eternal presence, and their new creation through their transformation in the eschatological moment from transience to immortality. We might call it something like a universal, cosmic feedback process.

This eschatological model for 'the future of the universe' is the only model which perceives a future for what is past and express-es hope for the dead. All other models of expansion, evolution, progress, or the steady state universe expect a future only in the sphere of what is not yet, but not a future in the sphere of what no longer is. They leave the past behind and gaze merely into the 'far-future universe'. But the eschatological model of the future brings hope into remembrance, and discovers future for the universe in all the stages of its past.

5. Two Open Questions

(a) Is the Universe Unique? And is Every Event Singular?

'Why is there something and not nothing?' That is the child's metaphysical question, and it is unanswerable. The universe is there as it is, but it is not necessarily there. What is there, evidently has a reason that is not inherent in itself but is to be found somewhere else. The universe is there, but it is not divine. This is expressed theologically not just through the concept of creation but also through the idea of the contingency of the world (*contingentia mundi*). It follows that the orders which we perceive in the universe are not eternal laws either; they are them-selves contingent orders.[23] The universe can therefore have different orders, and orders of a different kind. Natural laws are not eternal laws, like the Platonic Ideas. They can conceiv-ably change.[24] Consequently we recognize the natural processes in the universe through observation, experience and experiment, not through an ideal contemplation of essence. In the history of Christianity, the meaning of the term 'nature' has changed. It no longer signifies the essence of things, as it did in antiquity. Since the beginning of modern times it has come to mean their experi-encable mode of appearance. When we talk about 'the natural sciences' we are using the term 'natural' in a different sense from the way we use the word when we are enquiring about the 'nature' of things.

If we go a step further, we come up against questions about the experiences which we can prove scientifically. In a scientific experiment one can only prove what stands up to re-examination through repetition. But this means that only repeatable experiences can be 'proved', non-repeatable ones are unprovable. But in a world with an irreversible time structure, can experiences ever be repeated, in the strict sense? If in the universe there is no 'eternal return of the same thing' – if, as Heraclitus said, no one ever steps into the same river twice – then in the experimental repetition of an experience we do not come upon the same thing in the strict sense, but only something corresponding to it. The uniqueness of the happening and the experience remains. The great histories of the cosmos, such as the history of the universe and the evolution of life, are not repeatable. But perhaps on other planets we shall find comparable evolutions of life in stages different from those of the earth.

(b) Is the Universe a Closed System or an Open One?

Just as circular time was held to be the image and reflection of eternity, so the globe has been viewed from time immemorial as the image of perfection. In popular magazines even today we find not just the earth but the universe too depicted as a sphere. But a sphere is generally thought of as a closed system, and a closed system is thought of as a sphere. Yet if the universe has been involved in a unique movement of expansion ever since the Big Bang, then we should have to view the Big Bang as world middle-point for an expanding (and perhaps one day again contracting) world sphere, or we should have to abandon the image of the sphere altogether.[25]

All the systems of matter and life we know are open, complex systems. They communicate with other systems, and anticipate their possibilities.[26] Why should the universe as a whole, as the sum of all its parts and individual systems, be a closed system? We can certainly think of the sum of all open systems as a closed whole without affecting their openness. But we could also infer from the complex open systems a systematic openness of the whole which is not yet rounded off into an entirety, and has still not found a comprehensive organization principle for all the parts. All the formulae for the whole would then be anticipations of the not-yet-present and therefore not-yet-surveyable whole, and in so far they would be provisional and dependent on future confirmation.

If we follow the First Law of Thermodynamics, this idea about the whole as a closed system would seem to suggest itself, a system whose formula for the world we can look for and find, because it is bound to exist. If we follow the Second Law of Thermodynamics, and expand it into 'the theory of open systems', then what seems suggested is the idea of the open, unfinished and still incomplete universe.

Open systems show relatively fixed structures of reality, and relatively open scopes for possibility. They tend towards differentiation, towards growing complexity, and towards integration or networking with other open systems. They are open not only for quantitative developments but also for qualitative leaps in combinations into new wholes. Catastrophes and new beginnings mark their history more often than continuous developments.

That brings us to a final thought. If the beginning was marked by so unique and universally relevant an event as the Big Bang, is something corresponding then conceivable for 'the far-future universe'? An open universe would be open for the theological eschatology I have described; a closed and already completed world sphere would not.

VI

What is Time and How Do We Experience It?

Everyone talks about time: scientists measure time, historians are 'on the search for lost time', like Marcel Proust,[1] theologians talk about the presence of eternity in time, and about its future. In our everyday, colloquial language we say that 'we have time', or 'we haven't got time', 'we take time', or time slips away like sand in an old hourglass. Time seems to us long or short, it drags or flies, according to what happens in it and the way we experience it. We live in time and think in terms of time – and yet we don't really know what time is, because it is so mysterious.

In this essay I should like to approach the nature of time and the experience of time by describing and trying to compare the different concepts of time as we use them in science, history and theology. Between the concepts of time we find in physics (which I consider to be *non-temporal concepts of time*) and the theological concept of time (which I believe is a *temporal concept of eternity*) I shall go in some detail into the historical concept of time, putting it forward as the *temporal concept of time*; for I believe that here mediations between the objective time-measurements of physics and the subjective temporal experiences of eternity are possible. The highly complex time-concepts of human history in past and future allow us to arrive at a linked and common theory of time: this, at least, is my guiding assumption.

What I have to offer here is limited. I am suggesting that where the sciences are concerned on the one hand, and theology on the other, a historical theory of time can be considered under seven aspects. We can trace their origin in Hegel and Kierkegaard, and also in Heidegger, Georg Picht and Carl Friedrich von Weizsäcker.

I am starting from the concept of irreversible time, because that can be applied to natural and historical processes, and also to religious experiences in the three 'Abrahamic' religions, Judaism, Christianity and Islam.

Theologians belonging to these three 'historical religions' have always shown a predilection for the phenomena of irreversible time in nature, because their root experience, religiously speaking, is Abraham's and Sarah's experience of God – the exodus from country, friends, family, and the familiar natural environment into an unknown future of blessing for all peoples, the future which God promises. This experience of God is bound up with experiences of exodus and exile because it is aligned towards a new future through promise and hope. Anyone who follows this divine promise, and starts out afresh with such a hope, always leaves behind a past that will never return and to which he will never come back, and seeks a future that has never yet been. That person's present experience of God divides the times into a past that can never be regained, and a future that has not yet been reached.

If we compare this exodus experience in the historical religions we have named with Asia's great religions of nature and meditation, the difference in the understanding of time at once becomes patent: on the one hand the experience of reality as history, with an irreversible time structure – on the other, the insight into the greater and lesser cycles of the eternal return of the same thing; on the one hand the experience of existence in history, tensed between remembrance and hope – on the other the withdrawn and inwardly reposing Buddha, eyes closed, immersed in the inner experience of the eternal present.

Nature and history are not two different spheres of reality, as has always been assumed ever since the beginning of modern times. They are two different aspects of the one, single reality in which human beings exist and in which they participate. As Ilya Prigogine and his group of researchers have shown, this can best be seen from the transferability of the historical concept of irreversible time to certain natural processes: in all natural processes, in both mechanical and chemical reactions, we find temporal phenomena which can no longer be explained through the classic, geometrical models of equilibrium to whose equations past and future make no difference. In some scientific sectors – especially in open systems – we find today a transition from geometrical to historical models in which the dimension of irreversible time is fundamental.[2] When in 1953 Carl Friedrich von Weizsäcker called his book 'The History of Nature' (*Die Geschichte der Natur*),[3] he encountered protest from all the people who clung to the old, though false, dichotomies between history and nature – from mechanistically thinking scientists as well as from existentially thinking theologians, such as Bultmann. But if we admit scientifically that there is such a thing as a 'history of nature', we must on the other side also ask about 'the nature of history', and the characteristics and essence of historical time. And here we are using the word 'nature' in both the meanings familiar to us.

In his physics, Isaac Newton presupposed the concept of *absolute time*: 'Absolute, true and mathematical time flows evenly in itself and by its own nature, without relation to anything external, and by another term is called "duration".' This absolute time corresponds to Newton's idea of *absolute space*: 'Absolute space, by its own nature, remains without reference to anything external, always "itself" and immovable . . .'[4] The determining subject of this absolute time and this absolute space of the world is the transcendent God and Lord of the world.

Kant made of Newton's objective 'absolute time' his subjective 'transcendental time' as the condition that makes empirical intuition possible: 'Time is not an empirical concept that has been derived from any experience . . . Time is . . . given *a priori*. In it alone is the actuality of appearances possible at all. Appearances may, one and all, vanish; but time . . . cannot itself be removed . . . Time is a pure form of sensible intuition . . . Time in which all change of appearance has to be thought, remains and does not change . . . Time cannot by itself be perceived. [For] change does not affect time itself but only appearances in time.'[5]

The subject of transcendental time and transcendental space is the transcendental subject, in whom the intuition of the empirical subject operates. For Kant, in contrast to Newton, this means the human being as image of God.

But because historical time is neither absolute time nor transcendental time – because it is neither God's time nor the time of his transcendent image – it must be related to the experiencing subject, who is himself a historically changeable and hence empirical subject. If we start from this empirical subject, we see that there is a fundamental difference between the experience of time and the experience of space; for we can be in the same place at different times, but we cannot at the same time be in different places. We experience different times in the same place, but we do not experience different places at the same time, even if the modern 'spatialization' of the time-difference by way of TV, fax, e-mail and internet tries to make modern men and women omnipresent. The distance of the speed of light remains.

1. Present – The Mystery of Time: A Point in Time or an Instant?

In historical time we can distinguish between different modes of time. There is a before and an after, which distinguishes future from past at the interface of the present.[6] If we see future and past as lying on a single temporal line, then the present is a 'point in time' which distinguishes time's two modes, and at the same time links them with one another. This point in time is not itself a 'space of time': it has no temporal extension. It is a *punctum mathematicum*, a mathematical point. It is changeable, because it passes away with time, and at the same time it is unchangeable, because it is always the same. The present lies in time between the time of the future and the time of the past, and yet it is simultaneous to both these modes of time. Because the present 'point in time' distinguishes the times, it is also the end of time and its beginning, the end of the past and the beginning of the future.[7]

If we understand the here and now of the present, its *hic et nunc*, as constituting the times of future and past, we can also see the present as a category of eternity; for present establishes the unity of the times, and their difference. From this perspective, the point in time is the 'instant' which Kierkegaard called 'an atom of eternity'.[8] Mystical experience of 'the instant' has always understood it as *nunc aeternum*, the now of eternity. For even though the present is mathematically no more than a point of time on the line of time, it is nevertheless the time that is onto-logically specially marked out in being: only what is present *is* in the ontological sense. What can be in the future is not-yet; what is past is no-longer. So future and past are categories of non-being. Only present is the category of being, as Parmenides said in the famous Eighth Fragment: 'Nor was it ever, nor will it be, since it is now all at once, one, continuous.'

Theologically it follows from this that in relation to the eternal there is only a single time: present. Present is *the temporal concept of eternity*. We comprehend the past, which is no-longer, only through the force of remembrances which make it present, and the future, which is not-yet, only through the force of expectation, which makes it present. So both past and future are mediated forms of being. Only present can be experienced as immediate existence (*Da-sein* – 'being there'). And yet we have no consciousness of this immediate present, for every perception requires distance from what is perceived. Consequently our consciousness of the present instant is always too late or too soon; the instant and our consciousness of it are never simultaneous. In his philosophy of hope, Ernst Bloch talks about 'the darkness of the lived moment'. In his early, mystical period he called the same thing 'the darkness of the lived God'.[9] At all events, present is the inner mystery of the times.

2. Past – Present – Future: Reversible or Irreversible?

If the three modes of time are entered on an undirected para-meter, the movements which can be measured with it are revers-ible and symmetrical, as can be seen from the equations of motion in classical physics. If time is merely an instrument of measurement, it is indifferent towards the direction the movements take. 'Newtonian physics has the picture of the stable, reversible world, the world of a wind-up clock, a clock which can in principle even be made to run backwards.'[10] In complex systems *reversible* time secures stability, because it is the progressive form of cyclical processes, such as the rotation of the earth, the movement of the earth round the sun, the succession of the seasons, and so forth, processes which everyone can see for himself. Ideal symmetries are the circle and the sphere or globe. That is why we talk in this connection about the sphere of time, and speak of the globe when we are referring to the world. Reversible forms of time determine closed systems, symmetrical forms and states of equilibrium. Reversible time is a *timeless* time; for the form of time is itself timeless, like Newton's absolute time and the transcendental time postulated by Kant.

But with the Second Law of Thermodynamics the concept of *irreversible* time was in principle introduced into physics. Entropy is not merely the measurement for the irretrievable loss of energy. It is also a measurement for the irreversibility of processes. Warm becomes cold, but cold never again becomes warm. Fluxes of energy are directed processes, so their time is irreversible. Entropy was therefore increasingly used as a time measurement for unique, directed processes of this kind. And with that a first step was taken towards the awareness in physics of the temporality of time.

Ought we to work with both forms of time simultaneously, the reversible and the irreversible, and talk about a 'paradox of time'? Are there sectors in which the one rules, and others governed by the other form of time? Or can it be logically shown that the idea of a reversible time is an abstraction of a more complex process which follows the law of irreversible time? If nature as a whole is involved in a history, then the paradox is resolved in favour of the idea of irreversible time. The 'time arrow' then becomes the foundation for limited spheres of time.

3. Modes of Time and Modalities of Being

In the historical experience of time, the modes of time are not entered on temporal lines, in order to measure the quantitative differences; they are assigned to the modalities of being. Past – present – future correspond to necessary – actual – potential being. 'The possible corresponds precisely to the future . . . and for time the future is the possible.'[11] So what is future is possible, what is present actual, and what is past necessary, because it is unalterable. We can follow Ernst Bloch and assign the modes of time and modalities of being to each other rather more simply by saying that future is the sphere of the possible, past the sphere of the actual, and present the interface where the possible is realized or not realized.[12] At all events, the consequence is the irreversible 'time-arrow'. Future can become past, but past will never again become future. Potentiality becomes actuality but actualities can never again become potentialities. The modes of time, then, are not isomorphous. They differ in quality when they are assigned to the modalities of being 'possibility' and 'actuality'. Possibility and actuality are qualitatively different modes of being, and the way we deal with them is qualitatively different too. Remembered past is something different from expected future. It is fixed, and can never again be changed. Future, in comparison, is full of everything possible, so our expectations remain unsure. If, ultimately speaking, every actuality in history is realized possibility, then possibility is ontologically above actuality.[13] So among the modes of time future must have priority.

If we ask about the *source of time* – this must lie in the future. The irreversible arrow of time points out of the future through the present into the past. Yet the source of time cannot lie in *future time*, for all future time passes away. What today is future can tomorrow be already past. So we must follow Georg Picht in distinguishing between the future as a mode of time and the future as source of the times. As a mode of time, future time belongs to phenomenal time. But the future *of* time is present to every time, future, present and past. This transcendental future of time offers in a sense 'the whole of which the past is merely a part'.[14] The future of time is a reservoir of inexhaustible energy.

4. Remembered Past – Expected Future: The Introduction of the Subject into the Experience of Time

Once the subject is introduced into the experience of time, the particular phenomena of historical time come into being: there is no historical time without the experiencing subject. History is constituted through the remembrances, experiences and expectations of the suffering and acting subjects. This is true of human experience first of all, but not to human experience only, for every self-referential, open system of life perceives its time analogously.

In his psychological theory of time, Augustine relates past, present and future to the human soul's perception of them. Through remembrance (*memoria*) the human mind makes the past present. That is the past-made-present, not the past itself. Through expectation (*expectatio*) it makes present the future. That is future-made-present, not the future itself. Through what it sees (*contuitus*) the human mind perceives the present. That is the immediate present.[15] So in the human mind, past and future are in a certain sense present through the force of remembrance and expectation. They are even co-present. When remembrance and expectations are linked, a simultaneity of what is non-simultaneous comes into being in the human mind. In the human mind, through the force of remembrance and expectation, being-that-is-not-yet and being-that-is-no-longer are called into present being. These are creative makings-present of what is absent.

This simultaneity of past and future in the remembering and expectant human mind, however fragmentary in kind it may be, is a *relative eternity*, for one of the temporal attributes of eternity is its simultaneity. Universal simultaneity would be an absolute eternity as 'the fullness of the times'. The remembering and expecting present of the human mind can be understood as image and reflection of the absolute presence in the times of God's eternity. If through remembrance we call back into our present memory the being-that-is-no-longer of the past, if through our expectations we anticipate the being-that-is-not-yet of the future, this is a creative act of the human mind on what is absent and on non-being, and it is therefore an image and reflection of the God who calls into existence the things that are not. Augustine then also saw in these activities of the human mind the human being as image of God. Remembered past and expected future are joined by eternity made-present as their simultaneity. We can easily imagine the counter-check: without remembrances and without expectations we would have merely momentary impressions of points in time, but would be unable to perceive any connections or movements.

Yet there remain differences between experienced history and history itself. In the remembered past the difference between the past-present and the past-made-present remains. We remember only a little of the past. Our memory selects, and changes as time goes on. Our memory is not a computer memory. It is a living organism. In remembrance we try to come to terms with experiences which thrust themselves on us because they are still unfinished, have not yet been wound up, or still press upon us. 'Only what still hurts us remains in the memory', said Nietzsche. The painful remembrances remain until our memories are healed. We generally relate these recollections to ourselves, for they give us a picture of ourselves which can torment us or flatter us. Remembered past must therefore be corrected through the historical elicitation of 'things as they really were', as Leopold von Ranke put it. Here we are helped not merely by the study of documents, but also by comparing these records with the recollections of other contemporary witnesses. Past-made-present is stored up in the collective memory and its institutions too – or is falsified through collective suppressions.

Reinhard Koselleck has aptly talked about a 'space of experience' in which we collect historical remembrances.[16] As archives and museums show, these remembrances in 'the house of history' (as the German museum in Bonn is called) can be seen simultaneously and side by side, although they are in fact non-simultaneous and successive. Remembrance carries over the remembered times of the past into a common space of the present.

In expectations we make future present. We make it present not as future but as future-present, and as possible future experience. Here the difference between the future-present and the future-made-present of today is even greater than it is in respect of the past, and it is also different in kind. We have experiences –

we gather remembrances – but expectations are advance drafts. Experiences and remembrances are related to realities, but expectations reach out into the possible. These are different modes of being. So it is more appropriate to talk about a 'horizon' of experience, rather than a 'space' of experience.

How are remembrances and expectations related to each other? There are no expectations which are not based on particular remembrances and experiences, whether of things that have fallen short or of others that have exceeded our hopes. But we cannot derive our expectations from our experiences. 'Experience makes us wise', says the proverb – but not necessarily hopeful; for hopes can be disappointed and 'hope deferred maketh the heart sick'. Yet we cannot, either, draft our expectations without any reference to our experiences and remembrances. To do so would be to produce unrealistic utopias. The feed-back of expectations to experiences and remembrances is a necessary part of the hermeneutical process of tradition and innovation which makes up life. The presence of the future in the expectation is different in kind from the presence of the past in the remembrance. That is due to the qualitative difference between possibility and reality. In the awareness of historical time, expectations and remembrances are as interwoven as are 'the space of experience' and 'the horizon of expectation'.

5. Future in the Past – Past in the Future

The interweaving of the times in historical time goes further than we have described up to now. What we remember is not just the past of our own particular present but, to be more precise, the *past present*. But every past present, as it was experienced by past generations, had its own remembrances and expectations, and hence also its own interweaving of past-made-present and future-made-present. If we call to memory a past-present, we must also ask about its remembrances and expectations. With what historical remembrances and with what political hopes did the young generations of the European nations enter into the catastrophe of the First World War? What did the space of experience of the sixteenth-century Reformers look like? And with what hopes did they reform Church, state and society? What view of history did Luther have, and what apocalyptic expectations influenced his perceptions of the present and his decisions? Genuine traditions are always also remembered and passed-on hopes. In our own orientation towards the future we search for the hopes of the past and find them in the unfulfilled hopes and the still unpaid debts of the past generations that went before us. If we view our political histories, our cultural histories, and the history of humanity as still unfinished, unfulfilled processes, then we shall also take up the histories of hope which are bound up with them. 'The American dream' has still not been fulfilled. The vision of human rights and of democracy has not yet been realized. The hope for 'eternal peace' in the family of the nations which Kant voiced still beckons us after three hundred years. In this respect *the future of history* determines the times, and makes of the past past-future, of the present present-future, and of future times future-future.

6. Eternity in Time: The Temporal Concept of Eternity

The experience of eternity in time is nothing other than the depth-dimension of the present, because the present-in-the-mind, through the force of remembrance and expectation, establishes a relative simultaneity of past and future. If this takes place in one's own present, then it took place in past-presents too, and can also be expected in future-presents. Historical present always makes present past and future. Present in the mind therefore also makes eternity present, between the times of past and future. As long as it is 'today', eternity reaches into time. This presence of eternity in the historical moment is not the eternity of the 'Wholly Other' God, but it is the analogous, relative, participatory eternity of his image on earth.

The temporal concept of eternity is constituted not only by the simultaneity of past and future in the historical present, but also by the experience of past and future in 'the darkness of the lived moment'. This is the experience of the present as *kairos*, not as *chronos. Kairos* is 'the proper time', 'the favourable opportunity', 'the unique chance'. In the kairological understanding of time 'everything has its time'. Here the flow of time is non-homogeneous: there are favourable and unfavourable times. It is not homogeneous as it is in the chronological understanding of time. The kairological understanding of the present is heightened in the ecstatic experience of the present as 'the fulfilled moment'. This ecstatic experience of the present (which is also called mystical) interrupts the historical time-flow of future and past. In this experience remembrances and expectations vanish. We are wholly there, and forget ourselves and our temporality. Eternity in time is a category not of *ex*tensive life but of *in*tensive life. It is the experience of 'fulfilled time' in the totality of the lived life. If I am wholly there, I give myself wholly, expend myself wholly, am able to linger wholly, for I experience present eternity. It is to this experience that Boethius's famous definition applies: 'Eternity is a possession of life, a possession simultaneously entire and perfect, which has no end.'[17] Here eternal life has nothing to do with timelessness. It is fulfilled life in the experience of the moment. Experiences of *present eternity* such as this engender the longing for the *eternal present*. The fulfilled life in the lived moment makes us hungry and thirsty for the eternal 'fullness of life'. In the present of eternity we want to say with Goethe's Faust: 'O tarry awhile, thou art so fair.'

In the theological discussion, 'realized eschatology' was always contrasted with 'futurist eschatology', and often linked with the concept of irreversible time. The one is 'now already', the other 'not yet'. But this assignment to the different times is misleading; for what is 'not yet' can one day be 'now already', and what is 'now already' will soon be 'no longer'. What we are really looking at here is an eschatology of 'the present of eternity' on the one hand and an eschatology of 'the eternal present' on the other. The first is the anticipation of the second, the second is the fulfilment of the first. The realized and futurist options are not merely reconcilable. They actually condition each other mutually. Only they cannot replace one another. If the eschatological 'new creation of all things' brings the overcoming of transience by non-transience, it also brings the end of time. That means the end of this historical, irreversible time of *chronos*. But it thereby brings at the same time 'the fulfilment of time', which is the consummation of the *kairos* and of the presence of eternity in time.

7. Where Does this Reflection on the Nature and Experience of Time Come About?

Is there an Archimedean point at which we become aware of the temporality of life and the world? According to the classic view, this point is the death of the subject, because death is the exit from the time of life and the time of the world. Ever since the beginning of modern times, death has ceased to be viewed as the departure from time into eternal life; it is now seen as the departure into eternal nothingness. *Momento mori* teaches us to number our days and to use our limited lifetime. The making-present of our death in anticipatory awareness of it shows us, from our own mortal bodies, where time's frontier lies. If we take death in itself as starting point for the understanding of time, negative theories of time result. For the departure from time through death into nothingness manifests to us, theologically speaking, transience as the consequence of sin, of separation from God and his life-giving eternal Spirit. The experience of temporal life looks completely different if the departure from time is experienced in the fulfilled moment of present eternity. Then eternal life already begins here and now in the midst of transitory time. On the basis of this ecstatic experience of the present, death is expected, not as the departure from time into eternal nothingness, but as the beginning of that transformation into eternal life which will be consummated with the resurrection of the dead.

In the light of this expectation of resurrection, the essence of time is defined not as transience but as *futurity*, and in the corresponding 'rebirth to a living hope' it is expected, experienced and recollected as the history of the future.[18]

VII

The Origin and Completion of Time in the Primordial and in the Eschatological Moment

Eschatology between Eternity and Future

The history of modern theological eschatology is generally presented as the antithesis between consistently futurist eschatology (as represented by Johannes Weiss and Albert Schweitzer) and realized eschatology (C. H. Dodd and Rudolf Bultmann). It was considered that the two schools of thought could be reconciled according to the familiar mediating pattern 'both – and' and 'at one and the same time', and that this offered the true solution for the eschatological riddle. 'The kingdom of God' – the quintessential subject of eschatology – is both 'already' present in hidden form, and also 'not yet' present in its full, visible form. That is to say, it is 'at one and the same time' there and not there. (This was the position of Oscar Cullmann, Werner G. Kümmel and Walter Kreck.)

According to these ideas, the present and future of the kingdom of God are entered on the same temporal line: what is 'not yet' now, will one day be. But it is all too easily overlooked that everything that is already 'now' will one day be 'no longer', and that even that which is now 'not yet' will later on no longer be. These ideas about the 'now already' and the 'not yet' appropriate to the kingdom of God the quite inappropriate category of transitory time; and then the kingdom of God cannot be comprehended at all. This state of affairs was the result of 'consistent eschatology' – the result that shook Albert Schweitzer so profoundly: Jesus wanted to force the kingdom of God to come in his own time. 'This imperious forcing of eschatology into history is also its destruction; its assertion and abandonment at the same time.'[1] Instead of bringing about the eschaton, Jesus destroyed it once and for all. The expected end of the world did not happen. History continued to run its course unwaveringly. If we were now to supplement or replace this realized eschatology by a futurist one, the result would be no more than an apparent solution; for 'history' will catch up with every conceivable historical future, and turn it into the past. In this respect historical future is merely the future of the past. Unless the sense of time is remoulded, unless there is a new version of the concepts of time, eschatology in history cannot be conceived.

The real alternative to realized eschatology, to futurist eschatology, and to the mediating eschatology of a 'both-and' was the 'eternal eschatology' developed independently by Paul Althaus and Karl Barth after the First World War.[2] It is not 'history which continues to run its course' unwaveringly which leads every eschatological future hope into the deadly crisis of its disappointment; it is the very converse: it is the eternity of God breaking in 'from above' which plunges every human history into its ultimate crisis. 'We arrive at the completion not by traversing the longitudinal lines of history to their end, but by erecting everywhere in history the perpendiculars. That is to say, just as every time is equally close to the primordial state and the Fall, so too is every time equally immediate to the completion. In this sense every time is the last time.'[3] 'All the perpendiculars which we erect on the line of time in order to reach up to eternity, the parousia, the completion, meet in what is beyond time, at a single point. What divides itself up for us into a sequence of human death, the end of generations, nations, periods of time, is from this perspective the same act and the one simultaneous experience of the gathering up of history into eternity.'[4]

This 'gathering up of history into eternity' takes place in what used at that time to be called 'the eschatological moment'. The term has two direct sponsors: Kierkegaard, with his dictum that the instant or moment is 'an atom of eternity'; and Ranke, with his thesis that 'every epoch is immediate to God'. 'Precisely because it is the transcendent meaning of all moments, the eternal "Moment" can be compared with no moment in time',[5] for 'each moment in time is a parable of the eternal "Moment"'.[6] Before the overwhelming power of present eternity, all time differences disappear. Remembered past and hoped-for future are no longer there, for eternity has no time, and this vision of the eternal now, the *nunc aeternum,* swallows up all distances. Althaus calls this 'axiological eschatology'. With the help of 'the eschatological moment' of the present, Bultmann and Barth demythologized the Bible's eschatology of the end of history by interpreting it existentially and relating it either to the existence of the human being or to the existence of God.[7]

This eternity eschatology was of course not as new as it was proclaimed to be. Schleiermacher had already maintained: 'In the midst of finitude to be one with the Infinite and in every moment to be eternal is the immortality of religion.'[8] And even earlier Angelus Silesius had written:

> I am eternity when, from time set free,
> I join myself in God with God in me.[9]

Only Schleiermacher and Silesius did not call this eschatology. They called it mysticism.

The 'gathering up of history into eternity' does not merely lead to a de-historicizing of the biblical hope for Christ's parousia. It also means a de-historicizing of the biblical remembrance of Christ's death and resurrection. If the phrase 'the resurrection of the dead' is supposed to be 'nothing but' a paraphrase of the word 'God' (which was the way Barth interpreted it in 1924, in a reduction formula reminiscent of Feuerbach), then, on the other hand, the raising of Jesus from the dead too 'cannot be an event of historical extension side by side with other events of his life and death. The Resurrection is the non-historical relating of the whole historical life of Jesus to its origin in God.'[10] If God's eternity puts an end to history, then with eschatology it also puts an end to the history of Christ. Without a reshaping of the concept of eternity, eternity eschatology is a contradiction in terms. The 'eschatological moment' as it was formulated at that time permits neither the remembrance nor the hope of Christ.

Wolfhart Pannenberg's new 'theology of history' and my own 'theology of hope' start from a concept of the future which neither allows history to swallow up eschatology, nor eternity to put an end to history. This concept of the future is the advent concept of God's future. In Rev. 1.4 we read: 'Peace [to you] from him who *is* and him who *was* and him who *will come*.' We would actually expect 'and him who will *be*'. But instead of the future of the verb 'to be' we have the future of the verb 'to come'. The linear concept of time is broken through in the third term. With this a future becomes conceivable which does not bring future-past. God's Being is in his coming, not in his becoming (and his passing away). If God and future are bound together in this way, then God's Being must be thought of eschatologically and the 'future' must be understood theologically.[11] The future becomes the source and the meaning of time. It does not put an end to time, like eternity, and it is not absorbed into time as transience. It rather opens up the time of history, and qualifies this historical time to be the End-time. Because it is a matter of *God's* future, the times reach out for God's eternity, and this out-reach of the times is their future, a reaction to God's coming, and a parable of his eternity. Time is no longer the irresistible tow of transience and the triumph of death. And then future becomes a new paradigm of transcendence.[12] It is not just, in each given case, the temporal forecourt of the given present; it is the fore-court of past presents too. There is past-future, present-future and future-future. Eschatological future determines and ensouls all three modes of time.

But what, then, is the relation of this eschatological concept of future to the theological concept of God's eternity? How are eternity and time mediated to each other in the eschatological concept of future? We shall look at this question under four headings:

1. When does 'the resurrection of the dead' take place? On 'the Last Day' of history, or in the eternal Day of the Lord?
2. How ought we to think of the end of the world, if in that end creation is to have neither time nor space?
3. Does the End-time eschatological moment correspond to the primordial moment of the world's creation?
4. How ought we to understand the eternity of the eternal aeon of the new creation?

2. '. . . suddenly, in a moment . . .'

According to what Paul says in 1 Cor. 15.52, 'the raising of the dead' in 'the eschatological moment' at the time of the Last Trump will take place ἐν ἀτόμῳ, in an instant. There is no doubt that here Paul means 'the Last Day' in the temporal sequence of day and night, for this day does not come upon the dead only, but those then living as well: the dead will be raised, the living transformed. Yet the 'eschatological moment' of the raising of the dead does not merely take in all human beings at the same time, synchronically; it also happens diachronically to all the dead, beginning with Adam and Eve. Consequently this eschatological moment cannot be merely subsequent to all the days in the times; it must also be simultaneous to all days. This is expressed by saying that this Last Day is also 'the Day of the Lord'. If we look at it the other way round, then every day in time is in fact bound to touch this Day of the Lord. If that is 'the Day of Days', then all the days that come and pass away stand to this eternal day in a certain immediacy. But how can we think this eschatological moment of the raising of the dead as being at the same time End-time and eternal without the one dimension driving out the other?[13]

Mediaeval theological tradition tried to answer the question 'Where are the dead?' through the doctrine of an 'intermediate state'. In 1336 Pope Benedict XII rejected the doctrine that the souls of the dead sleep until the Last Judgement; so the individual hour of death and the Last Day of the world had to be thought together and yet in differentiation: after individual death, a particular judgement is passed on men and women. That is the individual anticipation of the universal Last Judgement. After this particular judgement the believer goes to purgatory (the state of punishment and purification) until in the end the purified soul, through the raising of the dead, is united with the mortal body, and arrives at the perfect contemplation of God. The doctrine of purgatory links eternity and the temporality of the eschatological moment, and also differentiates between them.

Because of the doctrine of justification, and because of the improper traffic in indulgences, the Reformers condemned the doctrine of the intermediate state. There is no time in the human sense between individual death and the day when the dead are raised. So Luther wrote:

> As soon as thy eyes have closed shalt thou be woken, a thousand years shall be as if thou hadst slept but a little half hour. Just as at night we hear the clock strike and know not how long we have slept, so too, and how much more, are in death a thousand years soon past.[14]

> Because before the face of God time is not counted, a thousand years before Him must be as if it were but a single day. Hence the first man Adam is as close to Him as the last to be born before the Last Day . . .
> For God seeth time, not according to its length but athwart it, transversely . . . Before God all hath happened at once.[15]

If the dead are no longer in the time of the living but in God's time, then they exist in his eternal present. From the individual hour of death until the universal Day of the Lord it is precisely a 'moment'. So the dead are already in the resurrection and in eternal life. Every believer dies into his or her raising to eternal life. The individual resurrection takes place in death. Consequently – so the argument runs – Christ says to 'the dying thief' on the cross: 'Today you will be with me in paradise' (Luke 23.43) – not in three days, not at the Last Day, but *today*.

Convincing though this interpretation of 'the Last Day' is for the individual, as far as the history of humanity and the earth is concerned it is still unsatisfactory, for it reduces universal eschatology to individual eschatology, and replaces the end of the world by the end of each individual. There is then no hope for this earth.

Modern Catholic theologians have experimentally developed a line of thought in the same direction,[16] and in doing so have come very close to Luther's view: God is not interested only in the soul; he is interested in the person's whole life. But during their lifetime people grow into the world, and the world grows into them. Sociality, bodiliness, the natural life: these belong to human existence. So, hope for salvation has to be comprehensive. And it is not 'the blessedness of the soul' that embraces the whole of salvation; it is 'the resurrection of the dead'. Because of this holistic view, these theologians call in question the idea of a bodiless intermediate state of the soul, and surmount the notion of a purgatory through the concept of 'the resurrection at death'.

Welcome though this attempt is, the reduction of the consummation of the world to personal consummation dissolves the community between human beings and this unredeemed world. If at our own death we were already to arrive at resurrection and eternal life, then we should be redeemed *from* this unredeemed world; for the world itself there would be no hope. But the phrase 'the raising of the dead' covers only the anthropological side of the eschatological hope for the cosmic 'annihilation of death' (1 Cor. 15.26, 55), and for a new earth where 'death shall be no more' (Rev. 21.4). The realism of the universal expectation of salvation requires a universal eschatology, that is to say an eschatology for the universe. 'Life after death' can be thought of only as the individual anticipation of the new future of the whole creation.

It follows from this that there must after all be an 'intermediate time' and an 'intermediate space'. Recent eschatology has always linked the fundamental idea of the anticipation of God's future in and through Christ with 'the eschatological proviso'. The intermediate time is the time between Christ's resurrection and the general resurrection of the dead. It is not empty time. It is not just a waiting room. It is filled with the lordship of Christ and his fellowship with the dead and the living (Rom. 14.9). His lordship arrives at its goal only when death is annihilated and he hands over the completed kingdom to God the Father. So those who die in faith die 'in Christ' and are 'with Christ' (Phil. 1.27); but they are not yet risen. They exist hidden in Christ's time and Christ's space, and with him go to meet their glory (Col. 3.3). The community of the living and the dead in Christ is a community on Christ's way to the new creation. In this community of eschatological expectation the dead are as little ahead of the living as the living are ahead of the dead. The images about paradise, Abraham's bosom and heaven, are probably not metaphors for the completion in the kingdom of glory of the new creation; they are figures of speech for the space of the dead in the time between Christ's resurrection and their own. The 'intermediate time' opened up and determined by Christ is to be understood as *End-time* not least because it is eschatologically qualified. And then the 'intermediate state' determined by Christ must also be understood as *End-space*, because it is eschatologically orientated.

3. 'The End of the World': Simultaneity and Omnipresence

What End-time means is described in the book of Revelation (10.6) with the image of the mighty angel who swears 'by him who lives for ever and ever, who created heaven and what is in it, the earth and what is in it, and the sea and what is in it: *time shall be no more*' (χρόνος οὐκέτι ἔσται).[17]

As the context makes clear with its invocation of the Creator and creation, *chronos* here means the time of creation, whereas eternity belongs to God. It is true that here the time of creation is contrasted with the eternity of God, but not as the sphere of the transitory over against the non-transitory. It is rather that time ceases once 'the mystery of God' is fulfilled (10.7). This presupposes that time was given and was there because the mystery of God had not yet been fulfilled.

I understand by 'the mystery of God' in this passage in Revelation the appearance of God himself to judge his enemies and to set up his kingdom. If God himself appears, then his eternal presence appears on earth too. Consequently the time of this creation then ceases and the new eternal creation is called into existence. If the eternally living God 'will swallow up death for ever' (Isa. 25.8) through his presence, then transience itself will also pass away (4 Ezra 7.31). But then the time of the Creator's long-suffering and patience with his creation ends too. The eternity of God will no longer concede time for the world and leave it time, as it has done since the first creation. If, in the new creation, creation-in-the-beginning is completed, then its time will be fulfilled. Its transitory time will be transformed into its eternal time. This is not the absolute eternity of God; it is the relative participatory eternity of those God has created. Patristic theology used the word 'aeon' for this eternal time of the new creation. It is a time without time, a beginning without an end – world without end. The proclamation 'time shall be no more' should not be heard in a merely negative sense, as 'the end of the world'. It ought rather to be understood positively, as the fulfilment of the time that reached out to eternity in the now manifested 'mystery of God'. The end of time is the beginning of the eternal aeon of the new creation. If this future of creation is revealed and opened up in and through Christ, then this time qualified through Christ is indeed 'End-time'. Because his resurrection from the dead is the beginning of the new creation, the end of the world is nothing other than the general resurrection of the dead, and the end of transitory time is the beginning of eternal time.

What *End-space* is, is described in Revelation (20.11) in a quite corresponding way. Before the erected throne and the revealed countenance of the mystery of God, 'earth and sky fled away and no place (τόπος) was found for them'. As the sentence shows, *topos* here means not a created place, but the restricted 'place of creation', whereas omnipresence belongs to God.

Before the unveiled face of God, earth and heaven no longer find any place of escape, and no space where they could remain. This presupposes that God concedes to his creation a space by 'hiding his face', and sets the limits to his omnipresence within which heaven and earth can exist before him in relative independence. But in the Real Presence of his unveiled, revealed face, this living space which was conceded to creation-in-the-beginning passes away. Then heaven and earth must pass away too (2 Peter 3.10–12), since no created being can look upon God and live. That is 'the future of the Day of the Lord' in its apocalyptic dimension. That is the negative presupposition for 'a new heaven and a new earth in which righteousness dwells' (2 Peter 3.13). The new creation is the dwelling place of God's righteousness. It will become the cosmic temple of the divine Shekinah. So it needs no space set aside by God for its existence, a space made possible by the omnipresent God's self-restriction.

The disappearance of the space of creation corresponds to the ending of time. Temporal and spatial distances disappear in the simultaneity and omnipresence of the Eternal One. The ending of both time and space take place in the *coming* of the eternal and omnipresent God, that is to say, in 'the eschatological moment'. Because the risen Christ is the beginning and anticipation of the new creation, he qualifies the time of creation to be 'End-time' and the space of creation to be 'End-space'. Like time, space too takes on apocalyptic features. Because the coming of the Creator's glory is in store for it, it becomes space that is open for God. The time and space of creation should be understood as aspects of the one, single movement of the coming of God, the announcement of whom sets them both vibrating with messianic expectations.

4. The Primordial and the Eschatological Moment

If we are to understand the eschatological moment, it is useful to go back to the primordial moment. The moment through which time enters into eternity is matched, in a mirror image, by the moment through which time once issued out of eternity.

The *primordial moment* lies before the creation of the world in God's resolve to be its creator. In this self-determination of God's is to be found the essential transition from eternity to time. In this resolve, God withdrew his eternity into himself, as it were, in order to take time for his creation. In the primordial moment, all possibilities are therefore gathered together and prepared which God will unfold in the time of creation. We can follow Orthodox theology and can call this the 'first aeon'. For out of this primordial moment in God the initial moment of creation proceeds. 'In the beginning' God created heaven and earth (Gen. 1.1). If the primordial moment is what Barth called 'the preparedness of eternity for time', then the initial moment is the issuing of time out of eternity in the very act of divine creation, through which the fanning-out of time into before and after, into future, present and past begins.

The *eschatological moment* should be thought of as a mirror-image of the primordial moment. God de-restricts himself so that in his creation he may become 'all in all' (1 Cor. 15.28). The time of creation ends – the space of creation passes away. Heaven and earth find their final form in God's presence. That primordial self-restriction of God's which made time and space possible gives way to God's glorifying *self-derestriction*. A new creation comes into being of which it can be said, in Dante's words, that 'His glory, in whose being all things move, pervades creation'. The transitory time of creation becomes creation's new eternal aeon. The space of creation becomes the cosmic temple for God's indwelling glory. The departure of creation from transitory time into the aeon of glory comes about through the resurrection of the dead and the transformation of all things. In the final aeon, all realities of the times which God created in the time of creation are gathered together. That aeon will see the restoration of all things, and the fanned-out times of history will be rolled up, as it were, like a scroll (Rev. 5.1).

The eschatological moment has two sides. In God himself there is his *self-derestriction*: God appears 'with unveiled face' in all his glory. He himself comes to judgement and to his kingdom. This is at the same time the fulfilment of creation's original goal:

the self-communication of God's glory. In creation *the kingdom of nature* and *the kingdom of grace* pass into *the kingdom of glory*. That is the end towards which creation-in-the-beginning was aligned and directed.

5. 'Eternity, time without time . . . Beginning without end . . .'[18]

It was always difficult to think time and eternity together, especially when time and eternity were defined over against each other through a reciprocal negation. So it is helpful to take up again the patristic concept of *aeon*.[19] Aeon is not the absolute eternity of God. It is the relative eternity of created beings who participate in God's Being. Aeon is time, but a time filled with eternity. The time of the angels in heaven is aeonic. The time of the new creation is to be aeonic – the time of eternal life which begins with the resurrection of the dead.

The essential difference between time and aeon is to be found in their respective movements. It is characteristic of the time of creation to be experienced through movement and change. Future and past can be distinguished through the before and after. From the *irreversibility* of future and past we perceive the 'ever-rolling stream' of time.[20] Time reaches out to the future. Time slips away into the past. These experiences make it possible for us to talk about linear courses of time, and to trace out their temporal lines either causatively or teleologically. Conversely, the movements from which aeonic time – time filled with eternity – is perceived are *circular*. For Plato the circularity of the times was already an image of eternity. According to Dionysius the Areopagite, the angels circle round the throne of God in heaven in spiral movements of contemplation and praise. They are changed from glory into glory without perishing, without growing, and without diminution. The *goal-directed* time of creation is consummated in the *cyclical* movements in which the eternal God is glorified in the new creation. The aeonic eternity of the new creation is full of mobility and vitality; if this were not so it would be impossible to talk about eternal 'life'. The aeonic eternity of the new creation is at the same time interpenetrated by the beauty of the eternal sabbath rest and its praise-filled joy in existence. Aeonic time is the answer to Nietzsche's saying: 'All delight longs for eternity, for deep, deep eternity.' For time makes all things old, and only eternity remains young.

VIII

God and Space

1. From the God of Hope to the Indwellable God

My early theological world was ruled by historical categories: promise and hope, protest and exodus, movement and liberation. In the 1960s we tried to break out of the narrows of existential and personalist thinking, so as to participate in the real human history of conflicts, sufferings and hopes. We discovered 'the God ahead of us' as the mainspring of world history. We experienced for ourselves the restless heart which refuses to be content with things as they are, but asks about a better future. Consciously or unconsciously, we were influenced by an accelerating history of revolution and repression in the Third World, and by the ever more rapid thrusts towards modernization in the industrialized world of the West – in fact by 'the renewing of the new' in politics, the economy and culture. These were the years of Pannenberg's theology of history, of my own theology of hope, of the theology of revolution and Gutiérrez's theology of liberation, of feminist theology and – in the wake of all these – the contextual theologies in movements for peace, for the preservation of nature, and for the liberation of the oppressed – movements finally given concrete and specific form in the prophetic kairos documents: theology at the right time.

It was only slowly, at the beginning of the 1970s, that we became conscious that human history runs its course within the ecological conditions of the earth, and that this means – as the Club of Rome made clear in 1972 – that limits are set to human growth. We were unwillingly forced to recognize that future in history too is not a land of unlimited opportunities. And with this recognition the all-dominating category of time became a problem. To put it metaphorically: we can 'move with the times', we can 'be ahead of our time' or no longer be 'in tune with the times'; but there is one thing we cannot do, and that is to stay put, settle down or rest in time. Time doesn't stand still. Anyone who makes history the symbol for reality as a whole must either historicize nature or naturalize history. Every comprehensive, unified theology of reality takes us beyond the category of time into the category of space – of place, orientation and stability, expanse and limits. We then arrive at spaces of time and space-times in our experience of the world, and at spaces of movement and life in our experience of living. But into what spaces does the experience of God lead us? And what ideas of God do we arrive at if we try to assess the spaces in God and God in the spaces?

Where do time and space meet, for us human beings? In everyday experience, we ourselves are the point of intersection between time and space, for we exist between the times of past and future, and between the spaces ahead of us and the spaces behind us, the spaces above and below and beside us – provided that we are aware of our present and have 'presence of mind' in the literal sense of the phrase (*Geistesgegenwart*, says German) – or, rather, are present in mind. For 'present' is not really a category of time at all. It is a category of space. The opposite of presence is absence. Only the people who are *there* are present, not those who are missing. The moment between the times of past and future is a point of intersection between time and space as well. So we shall not consider this intersecting moment only in terms of before and after, but also in terms of above and below, left and right, before and behind. We do not merely have presence 'of mind'. We are bodily present, and experience spaces with the body first of all, with its movements and all its senses, and not least with its feelings, above all the feeling of balance. How else should we find our bearings in spaces?

2. Experiences of Space

We shall begin with a little phenomenology of experiences of space. For unless we do that we cannot talk in a transferred sense about the spaces of God.

We are told that everything has its time. That is the *kairological concept of time*. Anyone who doesn't let things have their own time but snatches it from them, is aiming to fit them into his own time and subject them to his own power over time. In the same way, everything has its place, the place which belongs to it, and where it exists. That is the *ecological concept of space*.[1] Spaces are not homogeneous and the same for everything, as Newton and Kant assumed. Anyone who destroys the living space of other living things is letting them die. Anyone who makes them conform to his own environment and subjects them to his power over space is appropriating them. Every life has its own specific living-space. This is not something secondary. It is so primary a part of that living thing that we could also say the converse: that every living-space has its own specific living beings. The living-space moulds the unique character of its living things – the earth moulds terrestrial beings, water aquatic animals, and so forth. Biologically that is obvious enough. Even in the case of highly complex living things equipped with subjectivity, such as human beings, we see how a landscape, for example, can put its stamp on the people who live there.

Living-spaces belong to life. Free spaces belong to freedom. Spaces for movement belong to movement. Spaces of resonance belong to sound; and so on. These spaces are not just like containers, which may be empty or full but are in either case indifferent towards their content.

Human beings experience their space as both expanse and limitation. The 'wide open spaces' have become a symbol for liberty. 'You have set my feet in a broad place': that means, you make me free, and lead me out of constriction into breadth. The Hebrew word for 'deliver', *jasa*, means literally 'give space'. The wide space in which we can look out as far as the horizon is a physical invitation to move for ourselves, to step out, and to experience limitlessness. The wide space is an enticement to freedom: 'Go West, young man!' We can walk through the wide space, ride, drive or fly through it, but we cannot stay in it, or settle down in it. When evening comes we pitch camp and secure ourselves against the perils and dangers of the night. If we want to settle, live and sleep we need the restricted, enclosed space which protects us: the *boundary* then makes the difference between inside and out, home and the uncanny, our native land and exile, our own and the other. We need the enclosed, protective living-spaces which are familiar and trustworthy, and to which we can entrust ourselves.

Expanse and limit belong together in human life. It is of course modern to say that human beings are 'open to the world', as a way of pointing out that they are not just tied to a single environment. But no one can be permanently 'open to the world', and nothing but that. That person would be completely absorbed into the world, and the world would destroy him through the multiplicity of its impressions. Literally speaking, only the world-transcendent God can be 'a being open to the world', since it is only for God that the whole world can be a counterpart. We human beings can only afford openness to the world *within certain limits*, if we want to survive in the open world. Consequently we need the enclosed spaces which give us a sense of safe-keeping, which protect us and let us come to rest. The symbol for this is the dwelling place, the home where we can escape the homelessness of the desert. There is no human life without a home and dwelling place. 'Housing precedes life.' Everyone has a right to somewhere to live, says Article 25 of the Declaration of Human Rights.

But living-space must be understood socially and morally too, not just geographically and ecologically. In space, I look for and experience my place (*topos*), and in my place I experience, in Heidegger's words, *Dasein* – existence – as 'Being-in'.[2] I am *in* the world, *in* life, *in* my country, *in* my home, and socially I want to be 'in' as well. My existence 'in' something else or someone else is pre-eminently experienced as *social existence*: I am in other people and other people are in me. Every child grows for nine months *in* the womb. After it is born it grows up *in* a family. It lives, and later works, *in* society. To make this possible other people must 'make room' for the child – grant it a space in which it can live. If the child is to grow, its parents must withdraw; if it is to be free other people must open up free social spaces for it. If the young are to find jobs, the old must retire.

These social living spaces are supplemented by the *moral* spaces. There is no freedom without free spaces of the possible, so there is no morality either without 'moral spaces' – spaces for decision. In these moral spaces too we are both subject and object. *We* decide for *ourselves* and *others* decide for *us*. Our forefathers made multifarious decisions, and these condition and restrict our social and moral living-spaces. Because of the decisions already made in the traditions in which we exist, we act traditionally or innovatively, but never without these already-made decisions. I would call these social and moral living-spaces *perichoretic*, because their interaction – their warp and weft – their interlocking – goes beyond the simple subject-related ecological living-spaces. Every living thing has its space or home: *oikos*. Every living thing is a space for others: *perichoresis*. And it will be immediately clear that in saying this we are anticipating the doctrine of the Trinity.

How do we find our bearings in spaces? In terrestrial space we find these bearings through our bodies and our sense of balance. We stand upright because the body's axis is directed towards the centre of the earth. We can distinguish between above and below thanks to the earth's gravity. With our eyes we distinguish between in front and behind, with our hands between left and right. Through the perspective of our eyes we distinguish between near and far, through our ears we hear swelling and diminishing sounds. We are aware of the earth's space in the wider sense because of the earth's constant rotation. The compass points to the north, so we can measure latitude and longitude. The earth, for its part, is orientated towards the sun, round which it revolves in a yearly rhythm. Because this is true of the whole solar system, we can take our bearings from the fixed stars. The way this solar system is related to the other spiral nebula is something to be decided with the help of the Hubble space telescope and by way of gravitational and centrifugal-force calculations. In astrophysics we talk about a 'space of limited infinity', or about the 'curved space' of the expanding universe.

In the ecological spaces, ecological compatibility gives us our direction, in social spaces the compatibility with life which we call social justice. In the moral spaces we need the moral laws, from the Ten Commandments to the categorical imperative.

3. In the Spaces of God

(a) *Makom*

We find an early association between space and God in first-century Palestinian Judaism. *Makom*, space, became one of the names for God. In his book *Concepts of Space,* Max Jammer followed up this hint and found an elaborate history of rabbinic and kabbalistic concepts.[3] *Makom kaddosh* is the sacred precinct of the Shekinah. But used without a particular restriction, *makom* is a term for the divine omnipresence as Psalm 139 describes it. In the sense of a presence limited to his creation, God is understood as the *makom* of the world. This gave rise to a theological question that has still never found an answer: 'We do not know whether God is the place of His world or whether His world is His place.' The rabbinic answer was: 'The Lord is the place of His world, but His world is not His place.'[4] In the kabbalistic book *Zohar,* the Eternal One is called 'Place', since he is 'the space of himself'. *Makom* as a name for God also played a part in the great discussion between Isaac Newton, Henry More and Leibniz about 'absolute space'.

'You too he allured out of the jaws of fear into a *broad place* where there is no more cramping' (Job 36.16). In the language of the Old Testament, this broad place means the space of deliverance, a space in the undisguised presence of God, the living-space which delivered creation finds in God. Here again we find the two things: expanse and limit. The expanse of divine openness by itself would let every finite being drown in the infinite sea of the

Godhead. Deliverance would then be mystical dissolution. That is why we find side by side with the image of God as the 'broad place' the metaphor of God as 'the safe stronghold', as the place enclosed by God, protected, unassailable: 'The Lord of Hosts is with us, the God of Jacob is our refuge' (Psalm 46).

(b) Trinitarian Spaces in God

God is a spacious God, an inviting, ceding, delivering and finally indwellable God – not just supreme substance, not merely absolute subject, but also the living- space of his world, the space where those he has created can move, and their eternal dwelling place. Why is this so? Don't we find the deepest reason in God himself? God called to life the space of creation 'thanks to a possibility which was comprehended in his inner trinitarian nature'.[5] What possibility is this? If we think in strictly monotheistic terms, we should have to say: God is the space of himself and of those for whom he wills to be the space. But if we think in trinitarian terms, the wide space of God is more differentiated and more interesting. I am premising the foundation of the Christian doctrine of the Trinity in the Christian experience of God, and am moving directly into the innermost mystery of the Trinity, taking the concept of *perichoresis* for an understanding of its eternal life.[6]

John of Damascus (John Damascene) used the term 'perichoresis' for the mutual interpenetration of divine and human nature in Christ, the God-human being, and for the reciprocal indwellings of the Father, the Son and the Holy Spirit, following the pattern of Johannine christology: 'I am in the Father, the Father is in me' (John 14.11). In Latin, the Greek word *perichoresis* is translated by two different terms, *circumincessio* and *circuminsessio*. The first of these terms means a dynamic interpenetration (*incedere*), the second an enduring, resting indwelling (*insedere*). The Council of Florence (1438–45) provided the following formulation:

On account of this unity the Father is wholly in the Son, wholly in the Spirit; the Son is wholly in the Father, wholly in the Spirit; the Spirit is wholly in the Father and the Son. No one of them either precedes the others in eternity, or exceeds them in greatness, or supervenes in power.[7]

In their perichoretic unity the trinitarian persons are equal. There is no first, second or third Person in the Trinity. The words *incedere* and *insedere* show both the movement and the repose. *Circumincedere* says that each Person moves in both the others. They are the spaces in which that Person moves, in which it can unfold its eternal livingness. Every Person ek-sists in both the others – that is, it exists *in* and also *out of* (*ek*) the others. They are its living-spaces. It is love which allows them to go out of themselves to such a degree that each is wholly in the others. The Father comes to himself in the Son and in the Spirit, the Son in the Father and the Spirit, the Spirit in the Son and the Father. These are the trinitarian ecstasies. By virtue of their reciprocal indwelling, the trinitarian Persons join themselves to a unity and differentiate themselves mutually: the Father differentiates between the Son and the Spirit through his different relations to them; and so on.

Looked at in each case from the other side, the trinitarian Persons are not Persons only; they are 'spaces' for each other too. Each Person is at the same time the space for the movement, life and dwelling of the two others. Each Person makes himself *inhabitable* for the others by virtue of the perichoresis. That is the meaning of their *circuminsessio*. So we should not talk only about three trinitarian Persons. We have to talk at the same time about three trinitarian spaces.[8] Every Person indwells the others and at the same time gives the others space. The divine Persons do not merely 'empty' themselves to one another, as Hans Urs von Balthasar believes. They also mutually cede the others life and movement, and make themselves inhabitable for one another.

(c) God Becomes the Dwelling Place of His Creation

The God who within himself indwells so widely and in so reciprocal a way, corresponds to himself when he cedes his creation
space beside himself, before he creates it. God gives space, God
makes room, God withdraws in order to let a non-divine reality
exist with himself and in himself. This divine conferral of
space provides the free and open scope for the existence, life and
enduring being of those whom God creates.

In my doctrine of creation, *God in Creation*, like many other
theologians before me from Schelling to Emil Brunner, I took up
the kabbalistic ideas of Isaac Luria about *zimzum* – that is, God's
self-limitation for the sake of his creation.[9] Now I should like to
go a step further. According to the Kabbalah, the Infinite One
whose light originally filled all things, withdrew that eternal
light, and by so doing created empty space – space, that is, empty
of God. If space and light are equated here, what is being thought
of is not light as God's first creation (as in Gen. 1.3) but the
uncreated light of the Godhead itself. Through the self-restriction
of the Eternal One empty space comes into being – the *nihil* or
nothingness in which the Creator can then call non-being into
being. When he is about to create the worlds, God contracts his
own presence: '*Deus creaturus mundos contraxit praesentiam
suam.*'[10] The idea of *zimzum* probably goes back to the contrac-
tion of the womb at the birth of a child, just as the Hebrew word
racham means the birth pangs, and is only inadequately rendered
as compassion and mercy. Where God withdraws to himself
he can create something whose essence is not divine, can let it
co-exist with himself, give it space, and redeem it.

In fact what is thought of here in terms of space is only what
creation theology otherwise expresses in personal terms. If the
creation of the world proceeds from God's determination of
himself to be the Creator of this world, then here too God acts
first inwards on himself before he issues creatively out of himself:
God resolves for himself, determines himself, decides for himself.
Out of the whole wealth of his possibilities he chooses this one.
Translated into terms of space: God withdraws himself in order
to go out of himself. It is not his will to occupy the space of his

omnipresence alone. He limits himself in order to make room for other being.

In conceding space for creation God first frees a living-space in himself for the beings he creates. He determines himself to be the living-space for all those he has created. To take Plato's metaphor: God becomes 'mother space', the receptive and all-accepting one. Before the Almighty becomes 'creator of heaven and earth' he has already made himself the receptive and sustaining *space* for those he has created. Once we note this often overlooked side of creation, we find it analogously in all created beings: they are actively there, and are themselves passively received and accepted. Which side is more important is not established. But we perceive both everywhere. God cedes – God creates; God makes room – God calls into existence; God makes new – God allows a dwelling place beside him; God gives out from himself – God takes into himself.

When God restricts himself so as to make room for his creation, this is an expression not of powerlessness but of almighty power. Only God can limit God. God is only almighty where there is nothing. That is why the Creator of heaven and earth is called all-mighty. But where he has created something, God respects the unique character and the liberty of what he has created. Otherwise he would contradict himself. Only the relative self-negation of the absolute makes the liberty of the relative possible.[11] If this self-limitation of God's is true of his omnipresence, then it is also true of his omnipotence and his omniscience.[12] God has created beings with relative independence. By limiting his omnipotence, he has conferred the free spaces their freedoms require. Because of the restriction of his omniscience he cannot foresee how those he has created will decide, and how they will develop. He leaves them time, and opens for them an unforeseeable future. So he waits for those he has created, and awaits them. He is curious about the path they will take, for they are his future. He learns from them.

(d) Creation Becomes the Dwelling Place of God

But why does God give creation a space beside himself, making his eternal Being its dwelling place? We find one answer in the sabbath presence of God in time; another in the salvation history of God's indwellings in space: in Israel, in Christ, in the church, and ultimately in the earth where righteousness dwells – that is, 'on earth as it is in heaven'.

God's covenant with Israel 'I will be your God and you shall be my people' holds within itself a more profound promise still – 'I will dwell among the people of Israel' (Ex. 29.45). This promise of indwelling is the ancient language of the Temple, and yet it reaches out beyond all Temple precincts. We know the history of this indwelling in ancient Israel: first there is the transportable Ark of the covenant, in which, or on which, Yahweh dwells; then David brings the Ark to Jerusalem; and in Jerusalem Solomon builds for it his durable temple, in whose Holy of Holies Yahweh 'dwells' from then on. Then comes the catastrophe of 587 BCE, the destruction of the Temple and the people's Babylonian captivity.

This prompts the question: what happened to God's indwelling after the destruction of his dwelling in the Temple? Did it return to the unassailable heavens? That would have been the end of God's covenant with his earthly people. A more sufficient answer was that God's indwelling accompanied the people into captivity and helplessness, and into the exile of a hostile world. By virtue of his Shekinah, the Eternal One whom heaven and earth cannot contain becomes the companion on the way and the fellow-sufferer of his helpless people; for the promise to dwell among his *people* is earlier than the promise about Zion. God 'dwells' among the children of Israel even if they find no dwelling place and wander through the foreign land, despised, without a country and without a home. Whatever happens to the people also happens to the divine Shekinah that is among them (Isa. 63.9). The stories about 'God's self-humiliations' in rabbinic theology and in Jewish literature after Auschwitz apply to all these indwellings of God's.[13] If we take them seriously, we arrive at a bipolar theology: Where is God? God dwells in his own world, the world that corresponds to him 'in heaven' among the angels; and at the same time he is with the poor, the humiliated and the persecuted of this earth: 'I dwell in the high and holy place, and also with them who are of a broken and humble spirit' (Isa. 57.15).

It is easy to see that this Old Testament Shekinah theology is the root of the Christian experience of God in christology and pneumatology. 'The Word became flesh and dwelt among us' (John 1.14), for 'in him the whole fullness of deity dwells bodily' (Col. 2.9). But the experiences of God in the community of Christ go beyond the ancient Shekinah theology, because in these experiences the indwelling of God acquires a body, a name and a form: Jesus of Nazareth. If the experience of Christ is expressed through Son of man theology, we see this particularly clearly: the one who came to seek those who were lost gave himself up for lost in order to find them. From the manger to the cross Jesus had neither a home nor a country. He was forsaken and excluded. 'His own people received him not. But to all who received him . . . he gave power to become children of God' (John 1.11). And the people among whom he found a 'dwelling' were the poor, and little unimportant people.

In the fate of Christ the Shekinah is manifested as God's self-surrender, and the Shekinah itself becomes capable of suffering and death. What does this tell us about God? It says that the Creator doesn't just let his creation exist. He commits himself to it. He enters into it himself, so as to live in it; and that means to come to rest in it, and to remain there.

> O Thou whose glorious yet contracted light,
> Wrapt in night's mantle, stole into a manger . . .
> To men of all beasts be not thou a stranger.[14]

When it talks about the Word of God made flesh, Christian theology uses the word 'incarnation'. But in talking about the Holy Spirit, it speaks of 'inhabitation': the Word becomes life – the Spirit indwells. The Son of God becomes a human being – the Spirit of God indwells the many men and women who live in community with the first-born Son. From this point it is not difficult to direct one's gaze towards God's future, and to perceive the cosmic promise of which in history we always perceive only fragments. At his call, Isaiah sees 'the whole earth full of his glory' (Isa. 6.3). According to Paul, when the raised Christ has completed his mission, he will hand over to his Father the 'kingdom' he has gathered, and the triune God will be 'all in all' (1 Cor. 15.28). Then the whole creation will become his dwelling, God's cosmic temple. In the enduring presence of the living God, heaven and earth and all things will become new, and from this new creation death and pain will be excluded. That is the cosmic vision of Revelation 21: the world will become the living-space and the dwelling of the eternal God.

But that brings us up against the old problem:

Is God the space of his world, or is his world his space? If we say: the Lord is the living-space of his world, but his world is not his living-space, we put an end to Shekinah theology. If we pursue this answer in a Christian sense, like Hans Urs von Balthasar and Karl Barth, and say: creation is in God, but God is not in creation, then we do away with incarnation christology – or must replace it by an assumption christology: God was not *in* Jesus Christ but only 'assumed' him, for the Eternal One is unchangeable and impassable – incapable of suffering.[15]

But if we want to do justice to both *zimzum* and Shekinah, we have to hold fast to both these things: God makes himself the dwelling place for those he has created, and at the same time he enters into his creation in order to make it his own dwelling place. Is that a paradox? No, it corresponds to the perichoresis in its christological form: this is a reciprocal indwelling of the unlike, not the like. The world lives in God in a world-like way, and God lives in the world in a God-like way. They interpenetrate each other mutually without destroying each other. Is that a speculation? No, it is a daily experience of God: 'He who abides in love abides in God and God abides in him' (1 John 4.16). We remain in a human way in God: God becomes our living-space, our dwelling place and our free space. God remains in us in a divine way: we become his living-space, his dwelling

place and his free space. '*Ubi caritas et amor gaudet, ibi Deus est*'
– wherever there is love, God is there.

4. In a World between Space Travel and Homelessness

Practically speaking, we are doubly confronted today with the
question about space. On the one hand we see before us the
major project of modern times – space travel to other planets.
And on the other hand we are faced with the millions of migrants
without country or home, who find no space on earth where they
can live. The one is a marvel of modern science and technology.
The other is the greatest scandal of the overpopulation of the
earth and of an inhumane politics.

Why the one – why the other?

To explore space is an age-old longing on the part of human
beings. The observation of the stars and the search for the laws
ordering them does not merely satisfy curiosity. It also helps us to
understand the natural orders on earth, and the place of the earth
in the universe as a whole – that is to say, it is the orientation
required for living. But the modern transition from a closed
cosmos to an infinite universe destroyed the ancient sense of
being at home in the cosmic harmony. The gaze into the infinite
stellar spaces and the age-old times from which background radi-
ation reaches us awakens in modern people nihilistic feelings
of lostness and a transcendent homelessness. Pascal already
acknowledged that 'the eternal silence of these infinite spaces
frightens me'.[16] Nietzsche followed him: 'Are we not straying
through an infinite nothingness? Do we not feel the breath of
empty space?'[17] So are we existing on a little earthly island of
meaning in a cosmic ocean of senselessness which surrounds us
on every side? In that case we are not enclosed in a cosmos at
all, in the Greek sense of an ordered and harmonious system. We
are existing in chaotic expanses of rubble left behind by a
meaningless Big Bang.

But then what drives us to space travel today? Apart from
military utility in the struggle for power we call star wars, it is the

search for other intelligent beings on other planets where life is possible. We are searching for them because on the earth we feel as lonely as Robinson Crusoe on his island. The numerous space-probes that are sent out also contribute to the attempt to found human colonies on neighbouring planets with the help of space-ships. But what is the point? Are some of our contemporaries looking for a second earth to which they can retire when there is no longer enough living-space on this earth? Having, most unfortunately, destroyed this earth, we still have a way of escape which will allow us to survive. Or is this advance future plan-ning? We intelligent beings have conquered the earth, so we shall go on developing ourselves further through genetic engineering and with the help of our computers, and will turn from being earth-dwellers into citizens of the cosmos who will conquer the universe. Notions of this kind certainly exist, and not just in science fiction; they are evident even in the motives and inten-tions of science itself, as can be seen from the NASA applications for research funding.

If the space travel projects are being driven forward by these secret desires of humanity, then these desires can quite properly be characterized as an inhuman God-complex. If to be finite and earth-bound is something we can no longer endure, then we must break down frontiers and become omnipresent and immortal. But doesn't the speed of light, with its 300,000 km per second, set a definitive limit? No, apparently it is possible to get beyond this through curved spaces and 'black holes'. But what if we are not surrounded by a universe with a unified universal formula, but by a multiverse, or by unnumbered universes? What if we exist, not in a divine 'globe', but in open universal systems? Then even astronauts rushing endlessly through the spaces of the universe will not become gods. *Horror vacui,* the terror of space, is evidently an expression of fear for the God who has disappeared from his space, leaving literally 'nothing' behind.

Even though with the NASA spaceships we stand on the roof of the world, so to speak, when night comes we return to the world's underground cellars. The one watches the clock and 'hasn't any time', the other is on the streets and has no place. The person who is without a country is usually without a home too, the person without a home becomes restless and a stranger in a hostile world. To a large extent, overpopulation engenders the mass of surplus people who have to emigrate if they want to survive. Millions in the countries of the Third World have become migrants without either country or home. In the societies of the industrial West, the problem of the homeless is not a housing problem, or a matter of an 'overloaded boat'. This is an anti-social policy of pushing people out. There are 500,000 homeless people on the streets in Germany, and millions of empty houses and apartments where these people could live, but which they cannot afford. In the reports of an Open-Door community in Atlanta, Georgia, I read that (1) Housing precedes life, housing precedes employment, housing is a human right. (2) But keeping countless people homeless means that a cheap labour pool of disposable people is always available, because these people have no country, family, or other ties.[18]

Let me close with some questions about spaces.

Without space no human being can live. Are the homelessness of the streets, and the locked-up spaces of prison cells and forced-labour camps humanity's bottom line? Doesn't this mean that God, the indwelling God of the Shekinah, and Jesus, the home-less Son of man, are being pushed out of our world at the same time as these 'surplus people'? Won't God himself then become utopian, in the literal sense of the word – without any place? The Christian community will then become 'a dwelling place of God in the Spirit' (Eph. 2.22), and instead of the excluding spaces of the cold-shouldering society create inviting spaces for the Son of man, who is present in the hungry, the thirsty, strangers, the naked, the sick and the imprisoned (Matt. 25.35f.). It will be a home country for the God who in this world is homeless.

THE WISDOM OF
THE SCIENCES

IX

Humane Ethics and the Ethos of Biomedical Progress

1. Science and Interest

If science and ethics are separated, ethics always appears too late on the scene. It is only after science has taught us the methods of power that ethics are supposed to teach us power's responsibility. After the facts and the data have been listed, ethics are supposed to interpret them for people. Once the apparatus is at hand, ethics are supposed to ascertain its proper use, and prevent its misuse.

This pattern of discussion ends up in a cul-de-sac. From year to year we are better equipped technically to achieve what we want, yet ethically we ask helplessly: What do we really want? The greater the number of *possible* futures open to us, the less people seem to be able to agree about a common *desirable* future. The pressure towards progress in the sciences seems to make the humanities, culturally speaking, increasingly a matter of arbitrary choice. The mistake in this pattern of thinking is that it starts by *abstracting* science from society, and only then goes on to ask how to *integrate* scientific and technological power ethically and socio-politically into society's humane goals. But it is impossible to deduce any values from a value-free science, abstracted from values; so the values by which scientific results are judged land up in the arbitrary regions of existing social, economic and political interests, or of personal taste. On this level of discussion a great many ethical postulates can be set up and talked about, but they all remain without any relevance to actual practice, and are generally merely window-dressing for the show of public symposia.

In my view, however, this pattern of discussion has grown up out of an optical illusion. And I should therefore like to try out the reverse method. We shall begin with an analysis of the present ethos of biomedical progress, and shall then go on to ask about the repercussions of the progress on the ethos. We shall begin with the human and social motivations behind biomedical science and technology (which have not been very thoroughly investigated up to now) and shall ask how these motivations have been changed by the scientific results. In this way we shall reverse the theme; we shall ask first about the influence of human beings and society on biomedical progress, and then go on to ask about the influence of biomedical progress on human beings and society. It is only when we have come to discover the concerns that prompt this science's investigations, and perceive the interests that guide the application of these human technologies, that we can properly ask about the reciprocal effects of interests and knowledge in today's conditions.

The *segregation* of science from society, of science from the humanities and of technology from ethics was, and still is, necessary so that pure and applied science can be freed from the restrictions laid down by existing social systems of values and morals, and from social ideologies. Remembrance of the conflicts between the Church and science in the cases of Galileo and Darwin is still very much alive. And the clashes between state Marxism and the sciences in the Soviet Union showed that this liberation is necessary in other circumstances as well.

Today, however, the *integration* of science and society is just as necessary, if the sciences are to be freed from the new, quasi-religious roles which they have come to assume through their supposed separation from social interests and value systems. Once, the priests guarded the knowledge required for power from the laity. Today the experts have taken over this function – and the laity are in the same situation as before. This division of roles is a check on progress. It overwhelms the scientists with responsibility, while the fascination and horror exerted by scientific scenarios reduces the laity to a less than adult role. But the task of science can only be to make the possible decisions and their consequences clear, if these could not otherwise be discerned. This means that science itself is dependent on the dialogue between science and politics, and between science and ethics; for it is only through this dialogue that agreement can be reached about guiding interests, values and value-priorities. And here the sciences cannot be integrated into society unless society is integrated into science. We should otherwise find ourselves in conditions in which the planners and the planned, the makers and the made, are no longer, all of them, human beings, and when the objects can no longer recognize themselves in the subjects of science, and the subjects can no longer perceive themselves in the objects of science.

2. The Ethos of Biomedical Progress

Science, both pure and applied, is the response to a particular assignment. Human interests precede it, are bound up with it, and are incorporated in its progress. As long as these interests are self-evident, there is no need to discuss them. But in many sectors today the morality of 'what is self-evident' has become a problem. In the name of what human interests is this progress being pursued?

The invitation to the Hoffmann-La Roche symposium held in Basle in 1971 already said: 'The position of the firm (Hoffmann-La Roche) in the medical world has been strengthened in recent years because it views the fight against sickness and disease as an indivisible whole.' So our primary human interest is the fight for health against sickness and disease, and the struggle against death and to prolong life.

That sounds like a matter of course, as long as human beings are dominated by their natural deficiencies, which they have to counterbalance by cultural achievements in order to survive. But it becomes a problem once life's immediate needs have been met, and no longer provide the negative yardstick for human efforts. What comes after the struggle for existence?

The struggle for existence is linked with the basic concern of human beings to liberate themselves from their dependence on nature in the environment and their own bodies. It is the reverse side of their will to acquire power over nature and themselves. It is since human beings have emerged from their dependence on nature, and to the degree to which they have acquired mastery over nature, that they have become 'human beings' – that is, persons capable of action. Today it is becoming increasingly possible for men and women to determine for themselves not only their mental, spiritual and private life but their physical and social existence too. But liberation and power are only of interest as long as they are lacking. The more a person acquires them, the more the human qualities that have to be framed and lived become a question. 'What are people there for?'[1] Julian Huxley maintained that after the struggle for existence, what was now increasingly coming to the fore was 'the striving for fulfilment'– that is to say, fulfilment of human potentialities.[2] But which potentialities ought to be fulfilled, and which ought not? He added that for human beings the control of nature's evolution – or at least their own – was now going to become the inner determinant of their power and liberty.

For three thousand years the biblical religions have viewed the vocation to rule over nature as the fulfilment of human destiny; but they have linked that with the vocation to be the image of the creative God. They were not supposed to be the image of nature and natural forces. They were not to be an image of the destructive negation of being, and destroy nature and themselves. At the time when these insights developed, the possibilities open to human beings were few, while their dependence on impenetrable nature was great. In the wake of scientific and technological progress, human beings (if we see the matter positively) then began to fulfil these destinies in a hitherto undreamed of way.

The fundamental concerns for liberation and power generated a series of hopes in cultural history which were invested in biomedical progress. These hopes were directed towards the improvement of the human condition, a greater understanding of the world, the increase of humanity's capacity for happiness, and the raising of its morality. Out of these hopes, specific visions are being developed today, as they were, for example, at the CIBA Symposium in 1962.

1. The conquest of illnesses caused by viral or bacterial infection triggers off the vision of *a germ-free world*.
2. The development of psychopharmacological drugs is linked with the utopia of *a life free of pain*.
3. The growing technology of organ transplantation leads to the idea that parts of the body are replaceable, and to the notion of *an endless life*.
4. Modern eugenics make the control and *acceleration of human evolution* seem possible. This is associated with the vision that 'in the future people will create better generations of men and women' (H. J. Muller[3]).

On the foundation of these human interests, hopes and visions, biochemical progress itself is a splendid ethical undertaking on the part of humanity. But it only remains a living undertaking as long as these interests and hopes are self-evident.

3. The Repercussions of Progress on Ethical Interests

Every human action does not merely solve existing problems; it also produces new ones. Things usually turn out differently from what we had expected. These new problems can be divided into three groups:

1. Everything that can be used can also be misused. Consequently biomedical progress is ambivalent as long as men and women are unreliable beings.
2. Hopes can be disappointed if they are not fulfilled. But they can also be disappointed through their very fulfilment. The problem about the biomedical utopias we have mentioned – the problem, that is, for the ethics underlying them – is

not that they are probably incapable of fulfilment. The difficulty is that they probably *can* be fulfilled.

3. Every step forward in any sphere of life puts the life-system of the whole out of balance. So when any individual piece of progress is made, the balance has to be restored. The speech symbols, the legal codes, the morals on which we have depended, and the conditions of production must all be ordered afresh.

Looking at the first point: as long as the increase of power serves to overcome fundamental needs, it is obviously useful. But if it goes beyond what is necessary, it can be used in a way that is detrimental to life, and can produce new misery.

As well as the positive utopias we have mentioned, there are just as many negative utopias in the field of biomedical progress today. Biomedical progress may allow a public health service to be organized; but biochemical warfare is possible too, and so is the domination of a genetically highly bred élite over masses that have been reduced to idiocy by biochemical methods. Even if we leave speculations of this kind on one side: we can become more successful in the struggle against disease on the one hand and still ask, on the other, whether everything that is a good thing for the pharmaceutical industry is necessarily good for the rest of the world as well.

As regards the second point: hopes are generally disappointed when something different emerges from what we wanted. The liberation of human beings from their dependence on nature has not just surmounted natural deficiencies on the human side; it has also broken through a series of natural, self-regulating systems. These have to be replaced by social systems regulated by men and women.

Biology and medicine have reduced the death rate, but have let loose the population explosion instead. They have overcome a certain natural selection – but have exchanged it for a deterioration in the genetic make-up. They have fought bacteria and insect pests – but with DDT they brought about the 'silent spring' instead. They have fought pain – and created a world-wide drug problem. This liberation of human beings from nature forces us to undertake the social organization of that liberty, and this produces a multiplicity of new forms of social dependencies. The visions of a pain-free, endless, and improvable life in a germ-free world are abstract, because they do not take the social, political and ethical costs of such a world into account. Biomedical progress doesn't go along with any guarantee of happiness. Human progress is always unequal, non-simultaneous and unco-ordinated. It disturbs the traditional natural and social order and upsets its equilibrium, so that tensions and conflicts are the result.

In terms of *space*, biomedical progress has led to new social conflicts between rich and poor, men and women, the nuclear family and society. In terms of *time*, as Margaret Mead especially stressed, it has upset the natural succession of generations through a rise in the ratio of the old to the young on the one hand, and premature maturity on the other. In terms of *personal life*, it has disturbed the equilibrium of the self and the body, and produced new identity conflicts. A new social policy must establish justice where participation in health services is concerned. A generation policy must try to find a balance between an ageing population and population growth, so that the present is not sacrificed to the future, and the future is not sacrificed to the present – that is to say, that the old are not sacrificed to the young, nor the young to the old. We can no longer push responsibility off on to 'nature', or on to the so-called free play of natural forces either. What 'nature' once regulated through disease, early mortality and selection will now have to be taken over by human responsibility, through legislation and social organization. Intervention in natural systems has to be compensated for in other ways. This ecological law also probably sets certain tolerance limits to man's experience with himself and his future self-creation, if the costs of progress are greater than the returns.

Coming to the third point, however, we have to say that hopes can also be disappointed through their very fulfilment. If a pain-free, endless and improvable life in a germ-free world becomes possible, a human hope will have been fulfilled; and at the same time a dream will have come to an end. For it is questionable what meaning a life of this kind can have, and what people of this kind are there for.

Isn't a life without pain also a life without love? Isn't a life without opposition and struggle also a life without the experience of living? Won't an endless life be a boring life, without the character of uniqueness? Monotony, boredom and poverty of experience are already human problems today in industrial society, and have to be laboriously suppressed by means of new psycho-pharmacological drugs and psycho-technology. The more human concerns and hopes are fulfilled through biomedical progress, the more the ethical motivations that drive progress forward dissolve. People no longer know what they mean when they talk about 'I', or 'my body', or 'life', or 'death'. The consequence is that general interest in this progress can also ultimately flag and die out. Why should medical progress make people more efficient and productive, if most human achievements in this society can be formalized and taken over by machines? How can this progress make people more capable of happiness, when happiness can no longer be defined? It is not satisfactory to construct things which acoustically ejaculate the formula 'I am happy'. The more the humanity we have sought for up to now becomes possible, the more humanity has apparently to be newly interpreted and formulated, so that we can also do something meaningful with the possibilities open to us.

This is the question about the new balance in the life-system which faces us as a result of the outstanding progress achieved in the sphere of biomedicine. But first we must consider the question about the changes brought about by that very progress in the interests and concerns that prompt scientific discovery and practice.

4. Changes in Human Interests and Concerns

(a) From the Struggle for Existence to the Struggle for Fulfilment

'In psycho-social evolution the struggle for existence has been replaced by what might be termed the striving for fulfilment. The main operative agency in this phase of evolution is psycho-social pressure.' Let us take up this fruitful idea of Julian Huxley's as a way of characterizing the changes in human concerns brought about by biomedical progress. As a vision of evolutionary humanism, he calls the goal 'fulfilment': 'greater fulfilment for more individuals, and fuller achievement by more societies through greater realization of human potentialities, and fuller enjoyment of human capacities.'[4]

If the struggle for existence is replaced by the striving for fulfilment, people's concerns and their moral systems change fundamentally. The struggle for existence was a struggle for survival. In that struggle people were ruled by the negative things that threatened them – lack of food, sickness, a hostile environment, and competing groups. The meaning of their life was determined by self-preservation. But the more people acquire power over hostile nature and their own frail bodies, the less self-preservation and naked survival can be the meaning of their lives. The more they overcome natural deficiencies and produce an artificial wealth of possibilities, the more life in this wealth of possibilities becomes a problem. What was once self-evident, as necessary for life, loses its power as a stimulus once the necessities of existence have been overcome, or are at least no longer in the foreground. Consequently the evolution of the human being goes beyond the negation of the negative in the struggle for existence, out into a projected design of the positive, which is to be won from the superfluity of possibilities. This makes human life for the first time *de facto* a moral task. Once life itself has been secured, it is then a matter of the good and happy life in peaceful existence.

This by no means makes life easier, for now it lacks the clear standpoints and tasks that belonged to the struggle for existence. The hostile environment and hostile competitors no longer provide the negative yardsticks for the decisions existence requires. The goal of life's fulfilment and a person's joy in the play of his or her capabilities still point back to the life that was unfulfilled and restricted in the struggle for existence, and feed on the hopes developed there. But today these hopes are losing their power, as the spiritual helplessness of young people in the industrial countries already shows. The 'man of potentiality' is becoming what Robert Musil called 'the man without qualities'.

The more power the human being acquires, the greater his responsibility. So interest in self-fulfilment is inevitably bound up with responsibility for the sectors of nature which can be dominated. And because of its inner structure, responsibility *for* something is always linked with responsibility *to* somebody. And here the authority to which rule has to answer goes beyond the sphere of the thing *for which* we are responsible and can therefore only be postulated as something transcendent. I believe that for many people today – and especially for scientists – the 'pain of transcendence' is emerging at this point, a transcendence which demands responsibility and at the same time eludes the previous images and symbols. This pain of transcendence can provide an even more important impetus than psycho-social pressure. In view of the wealth of human power and potentiality, the Jewish-Christian symbol of the human being as the image of the invisible God in the visible world must also be newly interpreted today, if it is to be an effective symbol for human responsibility for controlling evolution in nature and the genetic experiments of human beings on themselves.

(b) From Social Darwinism to Peace in Existence

If the struggle for existence is being replaced by new destinies for human life, then the moral systems that have stylized the struggle for existence must be surmounted too. Forms of life can be developed which make creativity and love possible in rational world conditions.

The ethos of the struggle for existence must be changed into the ethos of peace in existence.

The principle of self-preservation *from* others can be transformed into the principle of self-fulfilment *with* others, that is to say, the principle of solidarity.

The systems of fear and aggression which were necessary for self-preservation can be phased out in favour of systems of hope and co-operation.

Today the group egoism which springs from self-preservation, and leads to competition and struggles for power, is threatening humanity with collective suicide. Even if that can be prevented, this egoism is already leading to societies of segregation. Wherever tensions and conflicts arise today, peace is established, not through reconciliation, but through division, expulsion, separation, apartheid and ghettos. Even without race and class conflicts, we are producing social divisions: the elderly in old people's homes, the sick in hospitals, the mentally ill in institutions, and so forth. Then the people who 'have made it' and got on in the world have things to themselves, and can divide up the spoils of the gross national product. Doctors estimate that about 50 per cent of the mentally ill would not have to be in hospital if their families would take them. But the urban social structure is intolerant. The same applies to the elderly in old people's homes. If in our society the struggle for existence continues in this hardly civilized way, even the capable will only be able to survive for a limited time – as long, that is, as they are neither ill nor old.

'Like draws to like' was the way Aristotle described the natural social principle. In our society today the effect of this principle is hostile to life, because it is divisive. Consequently *recognition of the other* is a principle that belongs to new human self-experience and self-fulfilment, so that people who are not alike can live together, and make their differences and divisions fruitful. There is no other way of arriving at peace in existence.

Finally, part of the ethics of the struggle for existence was the ideal of health in which health was identified with the capacity for achievement and enjoyment (see Freud). With this, health always ultimately amounts to unhindered participation in production, and undiminished participation in the gross national product. Sickness and old age are then merely evils which have to be repressed. The incurably ill and the old are treated accordingly, not to speak of the way (and the places) in which people die in our hospitals. A new view of sickness, age and death belongs to an ethics of peace in existence. For the person concerned, illness can be just as important an educative and formative process as healthy, active life. Our activist society has elevated youth into an ideal to a positively comic degree; now it is time to rediscover the dignity of age. Death has been viewed merely as a tiresome nuisance; now there are reasons for once more learning the *ars moriendi*, the art of dying, so that we may die with dignity.

The struggle against illness and for health is a good thing if it makes people ready to expose themselves to the human pains of love and the productive conflicts of life and death, so as to assimilate them in a truly human way. Otherwise the ethics of the struggle for existence would lead to a sick society. Where today this struggle is to a certain degree successful, it often leads to a life of stagnation, to a passive consumer attitude, without any passion for living. Where it continues, it leads to affluent societies set down on earth like islands in an ocean of impoverishment. It is only if an ethic of 'peace in existence' surmounts every ethic of struggle that we shall reach a state in which the healthy learn from the sick, the young from the old, and the living from the dying; when rich nations learn from poor ones, show interest in them, and feel solidarity with them because of that interest.

X

Science and Wisdom

According to the biblical traditions, *the fear of the Lord* is the beginning of wisdom. According to the early Greek philosophers, the root of knowledge is *wonder, thaumazein*, the Greek word meaning to contemplate with attention and personal interest. 'The origin of all philosophy is wonder', said Plato. So do we have to choose between Jerusalem and Athens? Must we decide between the Church and the laboratory? Have the sciences and the humanities over the years come to be two very different cultures? Are there two different windows on to reality? Or can astonishment over nature lead to the fear of God, and the fear of God to astonishment over nature?

It is possible to show in a general epistemology how recognition of the same and the analogous leads to a recognition of what is already known, and to its endorsement.[1] The repeatability of the recognition thus becomes the proof of its truth. Recognition of what is other and alien, on the other hand, gives us pain, because it requires us to change ourselves. By suffering what is other and alien we learn something, as the Greek assonance of *pathein*, suffer, and *mathein*, learn, suggests. But how do we perceive something that is new?[2]

1. The Root of Perception in Astonishment

If we encounter something unforeseen and unexpected, we are plunged into astonishment or terror. If we are astonished, our senses open for the direct reception of the impressions. Our attention is awakened, and we are intent with personal concern on what is at hand. The new thing that is perceived penetrates our sensory organs fresh and unfiltered. What we encounter makes an impression on us and we are im-pressed. 'We still can't grasp it', as we often say. We have been snatched out of our previous power of comprehension, and are at first bewildered. In fathomless astonishment, we are personally delivered over to what is new. That is why alarm and astonishment are so close to each other. In astonishment we open ourselves and give ourselves up entirely to the new impression. In alarm we draw back, and are concerned solely about ourselves. If we open ourselves to the impression of what is new, new ways of understanding emerge, so that we can retain the impression of what was new, and can remember it, and work on our new view of things, which corresponds to the impression in ourselves. The new impressions 'go on working on us', as we say. Perhaps we might call the perception that comes through astonishment *intuitive perception*.

In astonishment we perceive things for the first time. Astonishment is the only possible way of encountering the 'firstness' of a perception. The first time, we are delivered up almost defencelessly to the impressions. They overwhelm us. The wondering child still has no concepts with which it can grasp the impressions whose stimuli crowd in on all its senses from every side, for it cannot as yet remember anything comparable. It is only when the impression is repeated that remembrances are formed which allow the impressions to be grasped. Repeatable responses spring up to meet the impressions that crowd in. The child grows accustomed to the impressions and recognizes them. It knows about them, and is no longer surprised. The astonishment of the first occasion gets lost in what has become accustomed. The child has learnt. That is why we grown-ups think of wonder as belonging to the child's eyes, which see the world for the first time. Yet grown-ups who 'can no longer be surprised by anything' know that with every new child life begins afresh, and that every child discovers the world anew in its own way. The scientists and artists and thinkers we call geniuses have preserved childlike wonder more than other people, and the sense for the new and surprising. They are 'originals', because they have remained close to the origin of perception.

We go beyond childlike wonder when we say that the first perception of a phenomenon always evokes astonishment in everyone. Every new scientific 'discovery' awakens the astonishment that belongs to something that is 'for the first time'. Afterwards, these perceptions are repeated experimentally, and are absorbed as an expansion to our store of knowledge. But we are remembering 'the first time' when we label discoveries with the name of the discoverer. And here we can distinguish different 'first times': the first time of the perception, and the first time a phenomenon actually occurs. Because events of this kind evoke the astonishment over what is new, we talk subjectively about 'discoveries', meaning by that the disclosure of what has been hidden and the perception of what was previously unperceived. These discoveries can happen to us passively, and then 'our eyes are opened' or 'the scales fall from our eyes'.

Since the beginning of the modern scientific era, however, these discoveries are more often actively made.[3] People set out on voyages of exploration, or set up methodologically planned experiments in order to verify previous assumptions, or refute them. In German, one doesn't 'have' experiences; one 'makes' them (*Erfahrungen machen*). And this active 'making' of experiences has so strongly overlaid the passive experiences of events that the objective phenomena can hardly still be perceived at all. Scientific research asks: How does this function and what can one do with it? rather than about the nature of things, and the wisdom of their forms, and the warp and weft of their interweaving.

But every true dis-covery is also grounded in the objective side of the phenomena themselves. That is why we say that certain phenomena have 'revealed themselves' to us. Awaited but not forcibly elicited, they surprise us. We perceive what is shown to us, and our perception is prompted not by technical interests alone but by aesthetic ones too.[4] If we look at the passive and the active side of perception, we also find the consonance between that which has showed itself and that which was discovered. The discovery corresponds to the revelation; discovery and revelation are two sides of the same thing. We have perceived that which 'it was given to us' to know. We have found what we did not invent – it is a reception not an inception. We are astounded that it is as we have perceived it to be. To human reason there evidently corresponds a reasonable world. But what, then, is human reason, and what can be accounted reasonable? Before we go into this, let us look again at astonishment.

We are not astonished only by first-time events and perceptions. Even if we have already perceived something and are familiar with it, a trace of astonishment must accompany all our perceiving, for both in nature and in our brains nothing ever repeats itself in the strict sense, because time is irreversible.[5] What is past never returns. Consequently every moment in time is once-for-all. Only the astonishment in us has the power to perceive this uniqueness, this once-for-all in events and perceptions, for only astonishment makes us capable of observing the non-repeatability in what is repeated, the unlike in the like, and the dissimilar in the similar.

The person who has forgotten how to be astonished merely perceives as a matter of unthinking routine what seems to stay just the same. He expects nothing new. He reacts according to custom and doesn't understand anything. He judges 'what is the case' according to precedent, and screens out the once-for-all character of what has happened. By turning contingent events into 'cases', we subordinate them to some general rule in order to treat them all alike, as justice demands. But they are not all alike. Every case – we then realize – is different. Scientifically, we turn events into 'cases' in order to subject them to timeless natural laws. That too robs them of their contingency and uniqueness. It is only the modern chaos theories which again take contingency and uniqueness seriously. In art, in an age when all works of art are reproducible, we look again for the unforeseen, and produce 'events' and 'performances'.

If people turn into efficiently functioning creatures of habit, life passes them by, for every chance is once-for-all. There is no such thing as a second chance, at least not the same chance for a second time in just the same way. We might also call the attentiveness awakened and heightened by astonishment and wonder literally 'presence of mind'. It lets us 'take time by the forelock', as we say, taking up the way the Greeks pictured the *kairos*. To live attentively means to be open for what is new in the moment and for what is once-only in the event, and to experience life with tense expectation. If we expose ourselves trustfully to what happens to us, we dis-cover the new in the reality we encounter.

Every scientist is fascinated by the awareness that his object in nature is knowable. There seems to be a correspondence between human reason and the rationality of the world. Does the rationality of the world correspond to our reason, or can only the reverse be true – that human reason must try to correspond to the rationality of the world?

Modern scientific reason, according to Kant, 'has insight only into that which it produces after a plan of its own'. It 'constrains' nature to give an answer to human questions.[6] He compared a scientific experiment with the torture used to extort confessions. But this means that nature is knowable only in its reactions to human actions, but not in its own unique character. And then the question arises: what nature is it, that is the object of the sciences? The active, predatory reason which Hegel somewhat disparagingly called the intellect (*Verstand*) asks how the natural systems function, and what human beings can make of them for their own profit. The best way is to follow the old Roman method of domination – *divide et impera*, divide and rule, domination through division. If complex interdependent systems are investigated by reducing them to their atoms, and atoms by reducing them to elementary particles, these interdependent systems are individualized. The aim seems to be to reconstruct natural systems or to modify them. The image often used derives from the mechanistic nineteenth-century view of the world, with its construction-kit mentality. But it is only in our own imaginations that molecules look like pieces of Lego. Behind the image of the assembled 'parts' is the technological intention to reconstruct them, or to put them together afresh in line with human interests. It is a human image which we are imposing on nature, not the image which nature shows us of its own self.

In Germany today people like to distinguish between the

scientific knowledge which allows us to make free use of something, and the ethical-religious knowledge which lends orientation – the regulative knowledge about humane goals and purposes which nowadays seems to have got left behind in the wake of scientific progress. But this distinction presents the natural sciences and the new biosciences as if they were value-neutral: the values have to be tacked on later. But this is incorrect, for as the knowledge that provides power to dispose over things, the sciences already have clear, advance orientations: the will to acquire power over nature, the will to rule over life, and the intention to extend this power without limits. The modern sciences have been said to take the form of power. Consequently the modern discussions about nuclear research and the biosciences are based on two different and often contradictory orientations: on the one hand progress in the acquisition of power – on the other the ethos of human dignity.

It has often enough been remarked that while every animal's expert knowledge is confined to its own environment, human beings know more, and can know more, than they need in order to survive.[7] This instrumental reason – or so at least we initially assume – ministers to the power and progress of humanity. But what can we know and understand beyond that? Let us take as example the DNA analysis used in modern genetics: the genetic information in double track giant molecules can be investigated, so as to discover how they function and how they can be modified. At the moment this seems to be the predominant concern, not just scientifically but economically too. And this brings us face to face with an ethical question: can't we patent not just inventions but knowledge of the human genome too, bit by bit, so as to make a profit out of every bio-technological application of what is discovered?

Another kind of question arises if we note the experiences which are stored and passed on in the genetic codes.[8] We call this genetic make-up, but it is really more like a *memory* which has accumulated over millions of years in the sequences of these molecules. The systems of matter and life embody an age-old wisdom about life which enables affiliations hostile to life to be excluded, and others beneficial to life to be taken over. In this respect, research into nature is *research into memory*, and not very far removed from investigations into the cultural memories of the human race. The genetic information and the intellectual information given through socialization, language and imitation are not as far apart as the modern division between the sciences and the humanities seems to assume. For it is not only in human beings that genetic and cultural information slide into each other. How does the spider know how to build its web? Is a mother's love genetically conditioned, or is it acquired?

If, as we are assuming here, research into nature is the investigation of the natural memories inherent in the systems of matter and life, then we are investigating the *wisdom* embedded in the natural systems, and we do so in order to become wise ourselves. Then scientific reason is no longer merely a matter of the functional and dominating intellect. It is also a *receptive* organ. And if this is so, it should be possible to absorb instrumentalized reason once more into what the Greeks called *phronesis* – the all-embracing wisdom about life.[9]

2. The Fear of the Lord is the Beginning of Wisdom

We ascribe wonder as the root of perception to the child, and to the enduring, primal child in every adult. Wisdom, on the other hand, is something we expect of the old. They are supposed to have become wise through their experience of life and through the approach of death. But this wisdom doesn't come about by itself, simply with the years. Modern people become 'sixty years old, and not a bit wiser', to quote an old German pop-song, because their aim is to stay 'forever young'. But then how can we become wise?

Wisdom doesn't come from the experiences we have but from the way we deal with these experiences. It is not perception by itself that makes us wise. It is only the perceiving of perception. Wisdom is an ethics of knowledge. If we make a conscience of what we know, we become cognizant of our knowledge and our actions, and this gives us the chance to become wise. We look over our own shoulder, so to speak, asking: What do you think you're doing? What purpose is served by what you know? What has experience made of your life? What will be left when you die? Wisdom springs from a reflective counter-movement to spontaneous wonder and action. The wondering discovery of the world is one thing; wise dealing with what we discover is another.

We ask about wisdom in dealing with the divine, with the cosmic and with what is human, and we first have to ask whether these are quite different wisdoms, or whether it is a single wisdom which embraces these three dimensions and links them together. Here we are starting from the unity of what is different, because we are interested in community. We could also talk about the forms wisdom takes in these different dimensions, and would then arrive at different faces of the one same wisdom. We shall begin with the various special forms of wisdom in the three relations we have mentioned: to the divine, to the cosmic, and to the human, and shall then search for cross-links and interactions.

In *revelation theology*, it seems that God reveals himself in the events and persons of human history, and is then recognized again in nature. In *Wisdom theology*, God is perceived from the life and orders of nature, and then recognized again in human wisdom about life. Instead of God – human being – nature, the order here is God – nature – human being.

(a) According to Old Testament tradition, the divine wisdom is acquired by human beings 'in the fear of the Lord'. What is meant is not the *mysterium tremendum,* the awesome mystery which disseminates fear and dread. It is the sublimity of God which, when it is perceived by human beings, awakens reverence and humility. The fear of God links reverence in the face of the immeasurableness of the 'ever still greater' God with a childlike basic trust in his immeasurable goodness. 'To fear God is wisdom' and 'to love God is wisdom' (Sirach 1.16, 14). Fear and love describe the two sides of God's presence: distance and closeness, sublimity and intimacy, transcendence and immanence.

What kind of knowledge springs from the fear of God and the love of God? First, surely, a reflection about human beings themselves: Who am I? What is the human being? Before the sublimity of God, human beings become aware of their own nothingness, and all self-deification disappears. But in the love of God, human beings become aware of their importance for God, and all self-contempt disappears. The question 'What is the human being? isn't a helpless question, for in the Bible the question goes on: 'that you are mindful of him' (Ps. 8.1). So it is not just the love of God, it is also 'the fear of God' which is glory and exultation, and gladness and a crown of rejoicing (Sirach 1.11). The fear and the love of God are wisdom in the human being's relation to God. But what about the relation of this wisdom to God? In asking about the transcendent side of this wisdom, we are not asking about our wisdom in dealing with God; we are asking about God's wisdom itself. For evidently God is not just present in that wisdom, but the wisdom is present in God too.

The hymn of praise to wisdom in Proverbs 8 calls it 'the daughter of God', this being a way of stressing its divine nature:[10]

> The Lord created me at the beginning of his ways;
> before he created anything I was there.
> I was set up from eternity,
> from the beginning, before the earth.
>
> . . .
>
> Before he had made the earth or the mountains . . .
> then I was beside him like a master workman;
> and I was daily his delight, playing before him always,
> playing in his inhabited world,
> and delighting in the sons of men (vv. 22–31).

Here *pre-existence* is attributed to the divine wisdom. It is there from the beginning. God's wisdom accompanied God through all his works of creation, as his 'master workman', as his 'play', as his 'delight'.

The activities of wisdom here (as later in the book of Wisdom, chapters 7 and 8 too) are seen as being the forming, shaping and ordering of the divine works of creation. This may go back to the distinction the Priestly Writing makes between God's creating (*bara*) and his making (*asah*): in the beginning God '*created* heaven and earth' (Gen. 1.1) but at the end of this account we are told that God *made* heaven and earth (Gen. 2.4). The divine creating is incomparable, but the divine making finds its correspondence in the work of human beings (Ex. 20.11). For through his creative Word God 'called into existence the things that do not exist' (Rom. 4.17), and through the art of his wisdom he shapes what he has created, giving it its life-furthering form in the community of creation. An intermediary element between God's creating and his making is his *distinguishing*: 'And God separated the light from the darkness' (Gen. 1.4).[11] According to the book of Wisdom (7.17ff.), wisdom knows 'how the world is *made* and the power of the elements, the beginning and end and middle of times . . . the nature of animals and the tempers of wild beasts . . .' Wisdom knows this because she has made it herself and is present in the forms given to life. 'Wisdom is more mobile than any motion; because of her pureness she pervades and penetrates all things' (7.24). This is followed by an apotheosis of wisdom:

> For she is a breath of the power of God,
> and a pure emanation of the glory of the Almighty;
> therefore nothing defiled gains entrance into her.
> For she is a reflection of eternal light,
> a spotless mirror of the working of God,
> and an image of his goodness.

What does wisdom reveal about God?

For one thing, that God is 'a lover of life' (11.26). For another that he is the artist-artificer of this cosmos. He doesn't just call the world into existence, he also constitutes all things in such a way that they become the mirror of his glory. There isn't light and darkness in God – not creation and annihilation – not life and death. There is an unequivocal Yes and Amen. In other words, the transcendence is positively constituted. It is the transcendence of being, which shows itself in the existence and in the being-as-they-are of things; it is not a transcendence of nothingness, which manifests itself in the devastations of life and the annihilation of being.

Finally, the divine wisdom which interpenetrates, forms and sustains everything is more than created light, for it was there before light was created. It is light from the uncreated light of the Godhead, and communicates to temporal creation the eternal energies which are at work in the innermost essence of the triune God. As a creative force, it binds together the uncreated energies of God and the created energies of what he has created.[12] It is the divine mystery of creation, which finds expression in all created beings and in their relations to each other, and yet it is more than these. If this wisdom were not subordinated in the Old Testament to the fear of Yahweh, it might be compared with the Egyptian Ma'at, the *anima mundi* or world-soul of the Stoics, and the universal Reason of the Enlightenment. The book of Wisdom describes it in Greek-sounding terminology (7.25–26).

The cosmic wisdom tells human beings that 'The heavens proclaim God's righteousness' (Ps. 97.6) and that 'All his works give thanks to God' (Ps. 145.10). This means that a divine wisdom is inherent in all things and in their conditions and relations to each other, and that knowledge of these things makes human beings wise. Human beings can hear the hymn of praise sung by the community of creation and can chime in with it. A consonance can grow up between the cosmic and the cultural wisdom. This presupposes the belief that creation is in principle knowable by human beings. 'Through wisdom God has founded the earth' (Prov. 3.19). 'In wisdom hast thou made all thy works' (Ps. 104.24). His wisdom 'is poured out upon all his works' (Sirach 1.1–10). 'The whole earth is full of his wisdom' (Wis. 1.7). That sounds like the future promises of the Spirit that will be 'poured out on all flesh' (Joel 2.28) and 'the glory' of the Lord that fills the whole earth (Isa. 6.3).

We can conceive of this as being a graduated world-immanence on the part of the Creator: (1) in his works of creation through his *wisdom*, (2) in his works of sanctification through his *Spirit*, (3) in redemption through his *glory*. That would explain why wisdom is talked about pre-eminently in connection with human beings' dealings with creation, the Spirit pre-eminently in the sanctification of human beings, and glory in an eschatological perspective. Because the Old Testament texts are not interested in explaining their terminology, however, there are many over-lappings. But in these overlappings we can perceive the inter-twinings of God's immanence in the world; for in wisdom there is also an anticipated efficacy of the Spirit (e.g., Wis. 1.7), and in the efficacy of the Spirit – as Paul stresses – anticipated glory. So we can also say, conversely, that the crucified Christ manifests the divine wisdom (1 Cor. 1.18–24), because God has made Christ 'our wisdom, our righteousness and sanctification and redemption' (1 Cor. 1.30).

(b) That brings us back to the wisdom-structure of the created world. Confidence in a divine wisdom, which we assume is already given to us both in the cosmos and in the good life of human culture, acts like a pre-rational *postulate of scientific reason,* if this is on the search for wisdom. (1) The wisdom-structure in the build-up of matter and in the organizations of living things is an invitation to human knowledge, because it can be assumed that this structure is knowable. (2) The divine dimension of this wisdom immanent in the cosmos abstracts this wisdom from human knowing – however much wisdom may be known. That is the transcendent dimension of the immanent wisdom. This makes human beings humble with regard to what they know of the world: 'Wisdom is with the humble' (Prov. 11.2). Scientific humility means that in every extension of know-ledge we are aware of how little we know, because human perception and knowledge are realized in the wide space of the surpassing divine wisdom, and have their place in that.

If scientific knowing takes account of the transcendence of this immanent wisdom, it will take account of the unique nature of things. That is the hidden inner side of the outer side of things which is what appears to us. Kant still distinguished 'the hidden thing in itself' (*Ding an sich*) behind its perceivable mode of appearance. This *Ding an sich* is the true essence of things in the world of God, which remains inaccessible to the appearances of things in the human world, and which must be respected if appearance and essential nature are not to be confused. To perceive nature leads to the recognition of its own particular character. The interest that prompts and drives forward scientific knowing is then no longer merely the desire to dominate and appropriate the nature known; it is also respect for nature. We want to know nature in order to live together with it in the wise community of creation. We know nature in its interactions and interdependencies, into which we can integrate ourselves. This used to be called the 'sympathy' through which the divine wisdom holds all things together. The particularizing and individualizing methods of the sciences are then absorbed into the holistic ways of observing the wider connections between natural systems. This is successfully practised in the geosciences, in which geology, biology, and so forth, are gathered together. This does not mean any romantic dissolution of exact research, for the methodological doubt (*de omnibus dubitandum est*: everything must be doubted) has to be retained if sham solutions are to be excluded.

(c) In human wisdom it is a matter of distinguishing good from evil, preservation from annihilation, life from death. 'He who finds me finds life . . . all who hate me love death' (Prov. 8.35f.). We have said that the fear of God makes us wise in dealing with scientific findings. Then the scientific ethos is joined by the ethos which bears on the technological ways of exploiting these scientific findings. To the scientist's responsibility is added his or her responsibility as a citizen of his society and representative of its culture. The Greek *phronesis* distinguished between good and evil.[13] Jewish and Christian wisdom distinguishes between what furthers life, and the covenant with death.[14] For both, it is wise to make – or allow to be made – out of scientific perceptions only that which ministers to life, and to resist and renounce whatever spreads annihilation and death.

3. How Far Does the Responsibility of the Scientists Go?

For scientists in the twentieth century this question meant the question about war and peace. We can see the dilemmas involved if we look at two outstanding personalities.

The first dilemma was the one with which Albert Einstein unwillingly found himself confronted. His discovery of the general theory of relativity in 1907 was, as he confessed, 'the happiest thought in my life'. Its proof in November 1915 through the predicted movement of Mercury convinced him, as his biographer reports, 'that nature had spoken to him'.[15] This was in the literal sense pure knowledge, in proved agreement with what had come to be known. But then in 1937 came the discovery of nuclear fission by Otto Hahn and Lise Meitner in Berlin, and its application to an atomic bomb – an application which had been previously recognized and also already envisaged. The outbreak of the Second World War in 1939 raised the fateful question: the atomic bomb in Hitler's Germany or in the Western democracies? In his famous letter to President Roosevelt in 1939, Einstein made his decision. The Manhattan project began and led to the dropping of atomic bombs on Hiroshima and Nagasaki in August 1945, with the death of hundreds of thousands of people in a matter of seconds, and to the end of the Second World War. Pure knowledge and the wondering joy of discovery had ended up in the raw reality of the human struggle for power.

The other dilemma is summed up under the name of the German chemist and Nobel prize winner Fritz Haber. His discovery of how to isolate hydrogen from the atmosphere made it possible to produce artificial fertilizers in peacetime, and munitions in war. During the First World War, it was Haber's chemical researches and discoveries that made possible the German introduction of poison gas in 1915. For this he was ostracized by the international scientific community after the war had ended. The motto behind his scientific policy was a simple one: in peace for humanity, in war for the Fatherland. But his love for the Fatherland had its ethical limits. When the Nazis expelled his 'non-Arian' colleagues from his institute in Berlin in 1933, he himself resigned, and refused any further collaboration.

These two cases bring us face to face with the question: How far does the responsibility of scientists for their scientific research go – for their results, or even for that which they themselves or others make of their results? In normal circumstances their scientific responsibility extends to the methods used in their research. The direction of that research is not the responsibility of the individual scientist. The assignment is generally passed on to him or her by others, and is a matter for the scientific, economic and political bodies which make decisions about major scientific projects, whether these be nuclear power stations, the fight against Aids, or genetic engineering. But when a transition is made to the war economy, individual scientists too come face to face with the ethical question whether they are prepared to work on methods of mass destruction, or whether they should refuse to do so. If the use of modern methods of mass destruction, the ABC weapons, turn national wars into catastrophes for humanity, and if the survival or annihilation of the human race is at stake, aren't the people involved responsible for the actual construction of these weapons of annihilation, not just for their use? For the question about good and evil, life and death does not only arise for the first time when we ask whether these methods of destruction should be used. The question is already posed when the weapons are produced, or when those in power threaten to use them. In 1957 leading German nuclear physicists recognized this responsibility. In an official declaration in Göttingen which attracted a great deal of attention, they refused to co-operate in nuclear rearming – much to the annoyed frustration of leading politicians.

Of course this responsibility in its widest sense is not restricted to the scientists and technicians concerned. It rests on all the citizens of a society. Scientists are always citizens of their country as well, and share political responsibility. And if the whole human race is threatened by weapons of mass destruction, the responsibility rests on all human beings. Then, as I believe, the United Nations also has the right to intervene in those states which threaten the whole of humanity with these weapons. The community of nations must stop being a passive object of possible total annihilation through ABC weapons and become an active determining subject of our common survival. Through today's international war criminal tribunals, where those responsible for crimes against humanity and genocide are called to account, the community of nations has moved a step forward in this direction.[16]

In the last fifty years the ethical problems of responsibility for life on earth and the survival of humanity have been discussed exhaustively in connection with the production, use and control of these weapons of destruction. At the same time the 'peaceful use' of nuclear energy began, starting with the hyped-up promise of an 'inexhaustible source of energy'. Unfortunately scientists, technicians, politicians, and large sections of the public too fell into the trap of the sorcerer's apprentice: the formula for the industrial use of nuclear energy was indeed known, but not the formula for disposing of the radioactive waste. Because there is no disposal of radioactive material outside its mean or average life time, there can also be no 'final disposal point'. Every final disposal point is an interim point which has to be watched over for thousands of years, and every interim storage site today will have to act as an interim store for hundreds of years. An end is not in sight.

This sobering recognition should make scientists, politicians and the public cautious when the biotechnicians now claim money for research on the basis of similar extravagantly sanguine promises. Genetic modifications in plants, animals and human beings cannot be reversed again either, once they have been made. Genetic technology seems to be a technology as intolerant of error as nuclear technology.[17] Errors in both sectors have consequences extending over many generations – generations which have no voice today but have later to bear the costs. The sorcerer's apprentice couldn't console himself either with the hope that, later on, some more intelligent apprentice might perhaps come along with another formula that would break the spell.

Today the first power formula is in the hands of the sciences. The second power formula would be the one conferring ethical freedom over the physical power; and that formula rests in the hands of wisdom. We don't have to do everything that is do-able. Can does not imply ought! The power acquired must be used to benefit life and to hinder the destructions of life. That is the hour of wisdom, and the surmounting of the naïvely credulous faith in progress which can also be called foolishness.

For four hundred years human beings have set out to seize power over nature and life by means of science and technology. We now need a different time, in which human civilizations can be integrated into the geosystems of this earth. For we are part of nature too. We are not its godlike masters. The fear of God is beneficial in that it can free modern men and women from the 'God complex', as H. E. Richter called it, which in its disregard of transcendence has made human beings, in their lordship over nature, drunk with power and obsessed by the delusion of total feasibility. That is the religious side of wisdom. The fear of God leads to the ethical wisdom which makes human beings perceive their limits, recognize these limits, and thereby win power over the power of their science and technology. The last fifty years have brought such an enormous increase in our knowledge that what we need in the immediate future is a still greater increase of wisdom, and of wise dealings with what we know. For, to put it provocatively: the future belongs not to science but to wisdom – if humanity wants to have a future at all.

XI

'From the Closed World to the Infinite Universe'[1]

THE CASE OF GIORDANO BRUNO

Rome's ancient place of execution is today called Campo di' Fiore, and is a flower market. In this square is his monument. At the unveiling ceremony, on 9 June 1899, Professor Bovio proclaimed: 'Here he was burnt at the stake, and his ashes failed to quench his dogma. Here he rises again, and the religion of intellectual liberty demands no revenge. What it does demand is tolerance for all doctrines, all cults, and above all the cult of justice. Instead of the prayers of the Church, work; instead of mere faith, research; instead of obsequiousness, discussion. This religion's articles of faith are the discoveries of science, its concordats international conferences, and world exhibitions showing the results of shared labour. This faith has no prophets; it has thinkers. If you seek its temple, it is the universe. If you seek its sanctuary, it is the conscience of men and women. In Bruno's universe there is no excommunication, and to this congregation the whole human race has free access.'

1. Prophet or Heretic?

While many thousands streamed to the square, to honour the martyr of intellectual liberty and the religion of the universe, and to celebrate their own belief in work, science and progress, Pope Leo XIII spent the whole day on his knees in St Peter's, praying before the bronze statue of the apostle-prince, fasting, and fretting about the well-being of the Roman Catholic Church and its saving faith. Leo had also made a public statement on this occasion. His letter to all the faithful was read in all the churches, warning them against the arch heretic and heresy-monger, Giordano Bruno, and belittling him in their eyes. Leo wrote: 'He can neither claim any scientific achievements, nor has he acquired any merit through contributions to public life. His way of acting was insincere, hypocritical, and completely self-regarding, intolerant of any contrary opinion, totally malignant, and full of a coarse adulation which is a travesty of the truth . . .'

This remarkable catalogue of personal belittlement still finds an echo in the first edition (1930) of the Catholic *Lexikon für Theologie und Kirche*. There we can read: 'An unsteady, wandering life led this pathologically quarrelsome and rancorous man to Geneva, Toulouse, Paris, London, Wittenberg . . . whereby he did not hesitate to change his religious allegiance or cease from eternal wrangling . . . The spirit of the modern age, with its hostility to the church, sees in Bruno its chief hero, and has erected monuments to him in Naples and Rome.' The excitement seems meanwhile to have subsided and in the second (1958) edition of the *Lexikon* this personal denigration is dropped in favour of an objective account.

Is the judgement about Bruno at last becoming less prejudiced? Is his trial to be reopened, or are opinions about him still divided: on the one hand the free-thinking spirit, with hope for a humane world – on the other the faith of the Church, although overshadowed by the remembrance of Bruno's barbarous execution? Or are the heretics of old already tomorrow's prophets for the very reason that they were declared heretical? Did Giordano Bruno in his time really call Church and the Christian faith in question to such an extent that he became a mortal danger, and inevitably fell victim to what we may call – if we put it charitably – the 'self-defence' of the Church in Rome? Or was he the herald – far in advance of his time – of a new post-Christian, cosmic view of the world?

Bruno's indictment lists a whole number of 'errors', in part drawn from his cosmology of the immeasurable universe, and in part based on his satires on the pope and the Church. Condemned as an impertinent and obstinate heretic ('impertinente e ostinato eretico'), he endured cruel tortures heroically without recanting. His sentence was signed by the famous Jesuit cardinal Roberto Bellarmine. Bruno was handed over to the secular arm in Rome so that he could be burnt at the stake. But it was not the man alone who was burnt, but also – as the verdict decreed – 'all his books and writings, on the steps of St Peter's'.

Neither before or during his trial, nor since his death has Bruno and what he had at heart been taken seriously, theologically speaking. As far as I know, there were no theological discussions of his cosmology, and the people who took it seriously were not interested in its theological dimensions. If his world-view was pantheistic, materialist, and thus in the modern sense 'atheistic', why did Bruno talk about God at all? And why, then, did the contemplation of the immeasurable cosmos become for him the central experience of God? If he was forced by his view of the cosmos to talk about God, what was the nature of his concept of God? And what relation does it bear to the Jewish and Christian understanding of God's presence in the world?

In this chapter we shall look briefly at Bruno's life, and the basic elements of his world-view and his idea of the human being, so that we can then enter into the dialogue which theology has failed to concede him for the last four hundred years. That is the least which theology is in honour bound to do, as a way of restoring the dignity of this unhappy victim of an ecclesiastical fanaticism which, even though it was a feature of its time, is not out of the question even today.

2. The Life and Death of a 'Passionate Hero'

Giordano Bruno (baptized Filippo) was probably born in the spring of 1548 in Nola, at the foot of Mount Cicala, near Naples. On 15 May 1565, he entered the Dominican monastery of San Domenico Maggiore in Naples. The Dominicans were accounted the pursuers of heretics and witches. Scoffingly known as *domini cani*, the hounds of the Lord, they were at that time the executors of the Inquisition, although Thomas Aquinas had also lived and taught in the same Neapolitan monastery to which Bruno belonged. Bruno was ordained priest there in 1572, and it was during this period that he acquired his comprehensive knowledge of ancient and humanist natural philosophy. Apparently the Inquisition spy Montecalcini provoked him into entangling himself in rash debates. At all events, even then a secret file on him was opened, on the basis of which in 1576, when he was twenty-eight years old, the Inquisition drew up an indictment of 130 points, the charges being doubts about the faith and 'an inclination towards lascivious poetry', as the 1930 Catholic lexicon maintained.

The outlook for Bruno was hopeless, and he evaded the legal proceedings through flight. There began what German literature knows as 'Wanderjahre', years of apprenticeship. But they were neither unsteady nor volatile. They took him to what were then the intellectual centres of the European world. He travelled through Northern Italy, Venice, Brescia and Bergamo, and in Milan met the famous English humanist Sir Philip Sidney. In 1579 he arrived in Geneva, the refuge of Protestant fugitives from all over Europe. Calvin was already dead, Servetus's execution lay twenty-five years in the past, but in Geneva, with Theodore Beza, the era of Calvinist (Aristotelian) orthodoxy had dawned, and had already been the downfall of the empiricist philosopher Petrus Ramus, who was a victim of the St Bartholomew's Day Massacre in Paris in 1572. Bruno most probably joined the Italian Calvinist congregation in Geneva – at least his name appears on the congregational roll, as well as in the register of the Geneva Academy. But this is an error rather than the record of a change of religious allegiance: Bruno was a late Renaissance heretic, but not an adherent of the Reformation.

He soon moved on via Lyons to Toulouse, which at that time was the most important university city in France, after Paris. There, with a thesis on Thomas Aquinas and Peter Lombard, Bruno acquired the licence to teach theology, and began an extremely successful teaching career. One result will have been his writing *Clavis magna*, which deals with the mnemonics of Raimon Lull. 'The art of memory' always fascinated Bruno, and he himself must have had a phenomenal memory at his disposal. But there was more behind his study than that. His idea was to operationalize all the exercises of the mind along mathematical lines, and to make the human brain a thinking-machine that can be mastered. In 1581 he moved to Paris, became professor at the College de Cambrai, and won great esteem for his book on the art of memory, *De umbris idearum*, which he dedicated to the French king Henry III. In Paris he also wrote a number of literary works, including *Il candelaio*.

In April 1583 he moved to London, and lived as guest in the house of the French ambassador. During the summer of 1583 he held courses in Oxford on Copernican cosmology, and in the tolerant atmosphere of Elizabethan England, and under the protection of Sir Philip Sidney, wrote his cosmological works, *Cena delle cenire, De l'infinito universo et mondo* and *De la causa, principio et uno*. Though trying to imitate the style of the Platonic dialogues, he succeeded in writing didactic poems rather than genuine dialogues. He also published rhetorical writings, including the *Spaccio de la bestia trionfante* (1584), which – viewed as an attack on pope and Church – later led to his condemnation. His panegyric on the 'God-intoxicated' human being, *De gl'heroica furori*, appeared in 1585.

On his return to France in the same year, Bruno received an invitation to the Lutheran city of Wittenberg where, on the recommendation of Alberico Gentili, he lectured for two years on Aristotle. As thanks, in a final lecture he praised the German 'philosophical liberty' and Martin Luther. In 1589 he taught at the famous Lutheran university of Helmstedt, and wrote his chief works on cosmology, *De monado, numero et figua liber,* and *De immenso et innumerabilibus seu de universo et mundis* (1591). In the same year he taught in Calvinist Zurich. He had become a famous European figure, an internationally sought 'visiting professor', like so many 'outcasts' today.

Then, however, he received Giovanni Mocenigo's treacherous and fateful invitation to Venice, where Mocenigo soon denounced him to the Venetian Inquisition, which in 1592 had him arrested. That was the beginning of years of suffering. At the beginning of 1593 he was handed over to the papal nuncio, taken to Rome, and put in the prison of the Holy Office. His trial lasted for more than seven years, which suggests a skilful defence, and a degree of uncertainty on the part of the inquisitors.

The accusations against him were sweeping, as if based on suspicion: denial of the Trinity, identification of the Holy Spirit with the world soul (*anima mundi*), denial of transubstantiation and the virgin birth, assertion of the plurality of worlds, an atheistic conduct of life, ridicule of the pope and the cult of the saints, etc., etc. His defence, essentially, was that he was a philosopher, not a theologian, and that he had therefore argued on the basis of natural reason, not faith – both an Averroistic and a Lutheran two-kingdoms doctrine. In 1599, Pope Paul V – none other that the former inquisitor-general Camillo Borghese, in whose hands the trial had lain – actively intervened, and demanded that the investigation be speeded up. It was finally brought to an end by Bellarmine. In the papal year of jubilee 1600, Bruno was condemned. He answered proudly: 'You have passed judgement on me with perhaps greater fear than I feel in receiving your verdict.' The rest is atrocious and utterly shameful. Torn apart and lacerated by torture, he was dragged to the place of execution at dawn on 17 February 1600, and was burnt at the stake. His last words are said to have been the saying of the dying Plotinus: 'I am trying to take into myself what is most sublime and closest to God in the universe.' Bruno died with as much composure as Socrates, and as serenely as the Christian martyrs, in accordance with his own words: 'He who fears bodily pain has never shared in the divine.'

3. The Revolution of the Heavens

Until 1543 the Aristotelian and Ptolemaic world picture dominated the thinking of Europeans and their feeling about life. The heavenly spheres revolve round an immovable earth like spherical shells, and behind the sphere of the fixed stars lies the sphere of the *primum mobile*, the unmoved mover of the universe. In 1543 Copernicus's book *De revolutionibus orbium coelestium* appeared. With his mathematical calculations of the planetary movements, he put an end to the geocentric world picture. But it was Giordano Bruno who for the first time perceived the full implications of Copernicus's discovery, and drew the conclusions for cosmology. It was Bruno who first really brought about 'the revolution of the heavens'. He did not postulate a heliocentric world picture in contrast to the old geocentric one. He did away with centralism altogether, and had the courage to think the infinity of the universe and the relativity of centre and boundaries: 'There is neither centre nor circumference in the universe but, if you like, there is a centre in everything, and every point can count as the centre of some circumference or other' (*De l'infinito*, 5.2). The universe does not consist of concentric skins, like an onion. Rather, all the stellar worlds circle through immeasurable space. Only heaven is unique, the immeasurable space, 'the universal womb', 'the all-comprehending'. It is out of this space and the bodies found in it that the universe as a connected whole emerges. If, now, this world is in space, then there can be other worlds in this space too, and in innumerable other spaces there can be innumerable other worlds. Bruno initially meant by 'world' (*mondo*) only a planetary system, but his ideas on relativity clearly also put an end to the metaphysical idea about the unity of the one single world. And that meant that he had to recast the concept of God.

How is the absolute infinity of God related to the newly discovered infinity of the immeasurable universe? How is the unity of God related to the newly discovered plurality of worlds? Bruno was evidently concerned to clarify the differences between God and the universe: God is the confining, the world the confined. The world is infinite, God comprehends it, in the sense of the perfect totality and the complete being existing in everything. The universe has no *absolute* infinity, but only a dimensional one. 'I call God absolute and completely infinite because he is everywhere wholly in the whole world and is infinitely and completely present in each of its parts.' There is therefore no contradiction between divine and cosmic infinity. If God were merely another word for the universe (as the reproach of pantheism maintains), then the word could be dispensed with altogether, and the logical consequence would be atheism. But for Bruno, God has to exist because otherwise the universe is meaningless. Of course if God were no more than an abstract infinity, there would be no universe. The infinite would then be outside God, and would have to be an infinity of nothingness, as Spinoza later said. The concept of the infinite, omnipresent God makes it impossible to think the universe 'outside' God, and God 'outside' the universe. A God who has an 'outside' of himself would not be God. So the universe can only properly be understood 'in God'. Bruno by no means draws God into the world. He illuminates the world as being in God. If this world is immeasurable and dimensionally infinite, then the Deity, by existing, must be still greater (*semper maior*). That is to say, for Bruno the idea of God is indispensable.

But at the same time, for him the Deity is not merely the All-comprehending. He is also complete Being in every individual being. God is both maximum and minimum. If in geometry minimum is the point – if in physics the minimum is the atom – then in metaphysics, the minimum is the monad. All things are built up out of these primal units. They constitute the real unity of the world, for the Deity is the *monas monadum*, the monad of monads. Consequently, says Bruno, 'God is the monad, the source of all number' (*Deus est monas omnium numerum fons*). Just as the point as centre expands to become the circle, so the divine monad multiplies itself into numberless creatures. The protean world is the multiplication of the Deity (*multiplicatio Dei*). The greatest is inherent in the smallest, and the whole world is reflected in the tiniest thing. The vital germ of all things is in everything, and the striving for development and multiplication (*explicatio et multiplicatio*) thrusts every individual being beyond itself: a true coincidence of opposites, on Nicholas of Cusa's model.

Yet Bruno's universe is conceived of organologically, not

mechanistically, like Newton's. Consequently he takes up the old Stoic teaching about the *anima mundi*, the world soul, which was also familiar to the Fathers of the Church: the world soul, which gives life to everything, and moves everything, is the divine dynamic of the universe. 'Soul is to be found in all things, and there is no entity so tiny as not to have a share in it through which to be enlivened.' Like the Stoics and the Fathers, Bruno could also call the world soul the divine Spirit: the true reality and form of everything. With this he lent the universe a splendid subjectivity. This led to the idea that the world is a *living organism*. All things live with each other, for each other and in each other, in the community of the ensouled, organically formed and dynamically driven world. The universally efficacious unity is God. The all-interpenetrating power of life is divine: *physis optima deitas*, said Nietzsche: Nature is the best Deity.

Faced with the immeasurable universe, however, the human being loses all orientation. In immeasurable space there is no difference between above and below, right and left, in front and behind. From Pascal to Nietzsche, this shock was often described as the metaphysical homelessness of human beings. 'Whoever lost what thou has lost, stops nowhere.' Bruno took a different view. It is true that human beings are no longer the centre of a world made on their behalf, but for that very reason they can and must choose the centre freely for themselves and *create their own orientation*. Faced with the immeasurable universe, the human being, far from being lost, discovers his own dignity and greatness for the first time. Bruno is of course a man of the Renaissance when he calls the new human being in the immeasurable universe the 'passionate hero'. But he means the heroes of intellectual freedom and the fearless investigation of the universe, and the heroes of justice and truth as well. Their passion is a *divina strazione*, a divine torment, love for the divine in everything. Indeed in these heroes the divine Spirit itself lives and acts. They suffer the experience of primal Being: 'If God touches you, you will become flaming embers.' That is mystical ecstasy; but it is focused on the divine universe itself, not a God beyond the universe. That is why 'the passionate hero' feels that he is in profound harmony with the universe: in the finite he becomes one with that which holds the world together in its innermost parts.

4. 'Himself in all, and all things in himself'[2]

In the early years of the Enlightenment, Bruno's cosmological theses were discussed everywhere. His writings were present in the great cosmological discussions carried on by Newton, Leibniz, Christian Wolff and others. But his metaphysical world view only made an impact in Germany through F. H. Jacobi. Jacobi's treatise 'On the Teaching of Spinoza in letters to Mr Mendelssohn' (*Über die Lehre des Spinoza in Briefe an Herrn Mendelssohn*), published in 1789, which had as appendix a translation of Bruno's *De la causa*, kindled the pantheism dispute in Berlin and profoundly influenced the theology of the Goethe period. Goethe himself was not merely an admirer of Bruno ('that Faustian figure'), but was also an independent follower of his religious world-view. The best example is the Bruno-based poem 'Gott und Welt'. In his *De immenso*, I, 11, Bruno writes: 'There is no divine intelligence which revolves outside the world and pursues its revolutions, for it would be more estimable if it were subject to an inward principle of movement, so that we possess a nature of our own, ideas of our own, and a soul of our own, since these live as much in that innermost being as in the body, and with this are present in the generality of the spirit, the body, the soul, nature and ensoulment.' Goethe's version of this is as follows:

> Was wär' ein Gott, der nur von aussen stiesse,
> im Kreis das All am Finger laufen liesse!
> Ihm ziemts, die Welt im Innern zu bewegen,
> Natur in sich, sich in Natur zu hegen,
> so dass, was in ihm lebt und webt und ist,
> nie seine Kraft, nie seinen Geist vermisst.[3]

Goethe did not merely develop Bruno's metaphysical teaching about monads further. He also expanded his view of the world organism. Wherever there is an echo of Spinoza in early nineteenth-century German poetry and philosophy, Bruno is present too. In England, interest in Bruno was awakened by John Toland and through Jacobi. Coleridge evidently read Jacobi, and 'may have absorbed some of Bruno through Schelling as well as Jacobi'.[4] In the attempts already made in the early years of industrialization to overcome the mechanistic world picture on which industrialization rested, and to find a humane and organic relation to nature, Bruno was actually more important than Spinoza.

Today the theological discussion with Bruno has to be carried on under the impact of the ecological crisis brought about by the mechanistic world picture and the scientific and technological civilization which is based on it. The metaphysical precondition for the development of the mechanistic world picture was to strip the world of its soul. The old notion about a world soul, an *anima mundi*, was condemned as superstitious and animistic. The soul-less world was viewed as a machine ordered by God the Lord according to natural laws. Newton said that God ruled everything not like a world soul but like a Lord over the universe. The male concept of rule displaced the old female image of the organically ensouled world. That meant a fundamental change in the position of the human being in relation to nature. The goal is now no longer the 'passionate hero' who, in the divine Spirit, becomes one with the universe. It is now the human being who through science and technology makes himself the lord and possessor of nature. But if God's immanence in the world as Spirit is abandoned in favour of the transcendence of the divine ruler, the way is open for a view of nature which is through and through devoid of spirit and devoid of God. Then human beings take their leave of the cohesion of nature and the community of creation, and their civilization becomes a civilization actually hostile to nature.

But if nature and humanity are to survive on this earth, they must find the way to a new community with each other. Human beings must integrate themselves once more into the earth's cosmic setting. Human beings cannot integrate themselves into a 'world machinery' without surrendering their humanity. Consequently it is useful, and indeed necessary, to develop new ideas about the earth as organism, in the way that James Lovelock has done today with his Gaia hypothesis: people do not live *on* earth or *over against* nature, but *in* the earth as a total organism which through the constant absorption and processing of energy guarantees life in general, and human life as well.

The *metaphysical* foundation for a postmodern organological view of nature of this kind is without any doubt a new understanding of the activity of the divine Spirit in everything – to be more exact, in all complex and open systems of matter and life. The Cartesian reduction of the spirit to human thinking must be overcome, so that human thinking becomes a communicative thinking where nature is concerned, and no longer ministers to the one-sided domination of the human being over nature.

The *theological* foundation for the surmounting of the one-sided human lordship-religion of modern society is undoubtedly the rediscovery of the immanence in the world of God in the Creator Spirit, who calls all things into being and is for all the living the life that gives life. It was a one-sided, and not even a particularly ingenious adaptation of theology to the modern world when people maintained that 'the differentiation between God and world' was the successful achievement of the Jewish-Christian doctrine of creation. But creation is more than the creation of a work and God's self-differentiation from that work. The artist puts his whole soul into what he creates, and similarly God the Creator also puts his whole soul into each of those he has created, and communicates himself to all created being in his limitless love. The self-communicating Creator is present in all those he has created by virtue of his Spirit (Wis. 12.1), so that they are all able to love and praise him. Of course this does not make God and the world one, in the sense that they are one and the same. But God is nevertheless creatively present in creation in such a way that, with Goethe, we must see God *in* nature and nature *in* God if we want to understand the mystery of creation.

The justifiable fear of pantheism (which, as Schopenhauer said, is merely a polite form of atheism) must not lead to the destruction of the true pan-entheism, which we find in Bruno and Goethe. It is only if God remains God that his immanence in the world effects what is everywhere detectible: the self-transcendence of all open life-systems, their evolution, and their ever more complex warp and weft in relationships of community; for it is in this immanence that we find the 'more' which thrusts beyond every existing condition.

If, like the astrophysicist Erich Jantsch, for example, in his impressive book *The Self-Organization of the Universe* (1979; ET 1980), we say 'God *is* evolution', we should sink below the level of Bruno and Goethe, we would declare evolution to be the dynamic of the world, but would leave the dynamic of evolution itself unexplained. Out of negations can come only reductions. Consequently we gain nothing if, with Jantsch, we declare that God, *although* not the Creator, is still the Spirit of the Universe; but we surely acquire immeasurably rich perspectives if we say: *because* God is the Creator he is also the Spirit of the Universe. 'Spirit' understood as the dynamic of self-organization on the diverse levels of the universe does not become divine simply because we construct a dynamic concept of God for God, and call the dynamic God. Spirit becomes divine only through a concept of God differentiated in a trinitarian sense. It is only when we arrive at this horizon that we can say: everything is 'from God', everything is 'through God', everything is 'in God'. In these wider trinitarian complexes Bruno's vision also has its legitimate place: the vision of the immeasurable universe in the infinite God, the God who acts through the monads in the inner-most nature of the world, and the God who en-souls and totally en-spirits the universe. Bruno wanted to be a philosopher, so he made no use of the Christian ideas about the creation of the world, the incarnation, and the endowment with the Spirit. This is no cause for reproach, for in his time these theological doctrines were not offered to scientists and philosophers in so open a way that they could have been used in these other contexts.

Giordano Bruno is often said to stand at the beginning of the modern era, as a prophet of coming discoveries, and as a precursor for many others.

Giordano Bruno, as it seems to me, at the end of this modern era, returns as the herald of a postmodern 'paradigm' for a survivable human world in organic harmony with the Spirit of the Universe.

XII

Tao – The Chinese Mystery of the World

LAO TSU'S *TAO TE CHING* READ WITH WESTERN EYES

The *Tao Te Ching* has fascinated the European mind like no other Asiatic book. From Leibniz to Heidegger, philosophers have discovered here the purest non-Christian 'natural theology', or the true, general metaphysics. Martin Buber and Thomas Merton found in this book a unique religious mysticism, which takes its readers beyond all the established religions. More recently, deep ecologists and esotericists have become interested in the book, and use it in their own circles. Some Christian theologians in Germany discussed *Tao Te Ching* before the First World War, but little came of it. In this essay I am deliberately reading the book with my own eyes, exploring my own ideas about the different sayings, which were originally thought of as thought-provoking reflections, like the Koan sayings in Zen Buddhism. My intention is not to offer a historical-critical exegesis, nor is this an interpretation of the original meaning. It is the fruit of a mental and spiritual encounter bridging thousands of years and over immense distances in space and differences of culture.[1]

1. The Way and the Going

The whole content is already embedded in the title: *Tao*[2] is the mystery of the world which moves everything, and *Te* is the virtue which follows the way that is pointed, and is thus in harmony with the Tao. 'The greatest virtue is to follow Tao [the way] and Tao alone' (Ch. 21). The essence of the going is the going of it, the way of life. Western thinking has fallen on the mysterious Tao with all its own traditional concepts – meaning, God, principle, Logos, reason, the One, and so forth, and has failed to understand it. For the special thing about Tao is the very fact that it cannot be fixed and represented by any one human concept. If we understand it, we have failed to understand it. If we do not understand it, we are on the way to an understanding. We can say what the Tao is, we can say what the Tao is not; it is only by saying both things that we come closer to the Tao. That is why Lao Tsu says in his very first sentence: 'The Tao that can be told is not the eternal Tao.' Chuang-Tsu says: 'The meaning of which one can speak is not the eternal meaning.'[3] This is reminiscent of the religious art of mystical silence before the divine mystery, but it is not meant in this sense, for about Tao one must speak and be silent at the same time. This can be done if one's own speaking is continually caught up into silence.

[The way that could be shown would not be the eternal way.]
The name that can be named is not the eternal name.

The pre-eminent characteristic of the Tao is not to be a way that can be shown, and not to be a thing that can be named. It is an eternal way and an eternal name. In the first sentence in the book the negation that is bound up with its eternity can be related either to the human 'we' (because 'we' are temporal and mortal and unreliable, our ways are not the eternal, immortal and reliable ways of Tao); or it can be related to our 'speaking' and our 'naming' (it is not we who point Tao the way, but Tao that points it to us; it is not we who name its eternal name; it is Tao that knows our names). In both cases it is the qualitative supremacy of Tao above our existence and our actions that is stressed.

We are reminded of God's words in the book of the prophet Isaiah:

> For my thoughts are not your thoughts,
> neither are your ways my ways, says the Lord.
> For as the heavens are higher than the earth,
> so are my ways higher than your ways
> and my thoughts than your thoughts.
>
> (Isa. 55.8–9)

The word '*Ch'ang*' is used to describe the eternity of the Tao. This means the Tao's steadfastness and reliability. But it is also a way of saying that Tao determines everything but is itself determined by nothing – that is, it is an expression of Tao's supremacy and sovereignty. This is dialectically expressed by saying:

> The nameless is the beginning of heaven and earth.
> The named is the mother of ten thousand things.
>
> (Ch.1)

Or:

> Tao abides in non-action [The way is eternally without action],
> Yet nothing is left undone.
>
> (Ch. 37)

Although it is itself called unchangeable, Tao is nevertheless that out of which all change comes. Tao transcends space and time, and is yet simultaneously within space and time. Consequently it must always be described through negations and positions. This is finely described in Ch. 25:

> Something mysteriously formed,
> Born before heaven and earth.
> In the silence and the void,

standing alone and unchanging,
Ever present and in motion.
Perhaps it is the mother of ten thousand things.
I do not know its name.
Call it Tao [way]
For lack of a better word . . .

Tao is eternal and nameless, but when it begins to act, it has a name (Ch. 32). Tao is not, but when it effects being, it is. When it effects being, it acts through not-doing (*wuh-wei*).

Retire when the work is done.
This is the way of heaven.
(Ch. 9)

When Tao acts through not-doing, it acts freely and spontaneously through itself (*tzu-yan*). If it acts spontaneously through itself, then it acts without self-interest.

Heaven and earth last forever.
Why do heaven and earth last forever?
[Because they do not live to themselves
they are ever living.]
(Ch. 7)

Because of the way Tao acts, the *way* is in all things the 'essence' of things. But if their essence is not to be found in their transcendental Idea (in the Platonic sense), which is reflected on earth, but in their way, then this way must be understood as change and passage – that is to say, dynamically. The dialectical definitions which complement and negate each other, emerge from this: the name and the nameless, the non-being and the being, the acting and the not-acting. But is this then a 'way' in the biblical and western sense, with a beginning, a progression and a goal? Evidently not, unless 'the way is itself the goal'. In the Chinese Tao it is apparently a way which leads back and forth, or rather: oscillates between the poles of reciprocal negations and mutual complementations.[4]

[Truly, being and non-being spring from one another],
difficult and easy [condition] each other,
Long and short [offset] each other;
High and low [enforce] each other;
Voice and sound harmonize each other;
Front and back follow one another.

(Ch. 2)

These oscillations along the *way* are also described as 'Yin and Yang'. In this thinking, it is not the things that are primary, their movements and changes being secondary. On the contrary: things exist only in their transformations, as this text says with its 'springing from', 'condition', 'offset', 'enforce', 'harmonize' and 'follow'.

Is the Tao 'personal' or 'impersonal'? Christian theologians often ask this typically western 'either-or' question, because they would like to compare Tao with the 'personal God'. But the answer cannot be 'both-and', but only 'neither-nor'. Since 'person' is a term for the human being, it is not applied in Taoism to the Tao, for it is not the human being who mediates between the divine and nature, as in the biblical traditions, with their concept of salvation. It is nature which mediates between the Tao and the human being.

Man follows the earth.
Earth follows heaven.
Heaven follows the Tao [way].
Tao [the way] follows what is natural.

(Ch. 25)

Consequently nature is not absorbed into the human person. The opposite is the case: the human person is integrated into the Tao, which acts in all things. To live in accordance with the Tao means 'living in accordance with nature', a precept we also find in the Stoic Diogenes Laertes.

Non-being and being, the nameless and the nameable, the unutterable and the utterable in Tao makes the Tao the subject of

its own being, its own name, and its own utterance. The foundation for the being and the manifestations of the Tao in the world
are to be found in the Tao itself. In its non-being Tao is nameless
and unutterable, in its being it is nameable and utterable.

In contrast to all this, western philosophy, ever since
Parmenides and Plato, started from the Being of beings (*Sein des
Seienden*), not from the non-being of Being. Being is absolute
presence, it is never 'not-yet' and never 'no-longer'. It excludes
all non-being. Christian theology has always followed this Greek
metaphysics, taking as starting point the absolute being of God.
It was the problem of how to name and utter the divine which
first made clear the infinite difference between the finite and the
infinite, and the inappropriateness of all the names and concepts
conceived by the finite human being for the infinite Deity. Greek
tradition developed 'apophatic theology' at this point, western
theological tradition 'negative theology'. Both clung to the Being
of God, but found it totally impossible to grasp what the essence
of this Being is. All the names we give to God are drawn from his
works, which we experience; but they do not give – do not reach
– the essence of this Being. All human utterances about God are
no more than analogies, 'similarity in still greater dissimilarity',
as the Council of Florence said. John Scotus Erigena, however,
went further when he even threw doubt on the statements about
God's Being. Everything we describe and say remains within the
sphere of being. But the Deity is 'no-thing', because it is not itself
the Being of finite beings, but the Being of beings also derives
from it. Meister Eckhart followed him when he called the Deity
both the Being of beings and the nothingness of being.

What is this dialectic trying to say? Taoism says that Tao is
only known through Tao – Christian theology that God is only
known through God. 'In his light we see light' (Ps. 36.9). Does
this also mean that because God does not reveal himself directly,
he makes our ideas, names and concepts *analogies* for his own
Being, and through their mediation reveals himself indirectly,
metaphorically and through parables? Biblical theology talks
about revelations of God like this, revelations through human
mediations; Taoism does not. But Taoism also distinguishes the

nature of the Tao from its workings. The one remains in non-being and is unknowable, the other is perceived in all things and transformations. But this is a question, not of revelation and belief, but of *Te*, the virtue of the life that is in full accord with the omnipresent Tao. In western tradition this could be called a *unio mystica*, a mystical union, but this has then to be understood cosmically, not acosmically, as western mysticism has generally done, when it leaves the world of the senses behind, in order to seek the transcendent God in the self-transcendence of the mystic's own soul.

The non-being being, the nameless name and the unutterable utterance of Tao is fundamentally speaking more consistent than the category of analogy, which mediates between similarity and dissimilarity, for Taoism binds together contradiction and correspondence – indeed actually brings correspondence about through contradiction. In this dialectic, No and Yes are unequivocal, whereas the analogies of analogic theology remain strangely indefinite and cloudy. Similarity in existing dissimilarity does not say much more than: it may be so, but it may not be so as well. We say: 'God is our Father.' But if someone asks in return, 'Is he really?', the answer has to be: perhaps – we don't know – it is merely a religious analogy.

If we adhere consistently to the dialectic, we cannot stop short at the simple and non-dialectical distinction between the being and workings of the Tao; we have to say both that God's Being is his activity, and that God's activity is not his Being. In Christian theology both are also held to be true: in the act of proclamation God's Word is in the human word, and 'if you forgive the sins of any they *are* forgiven'; but in the act of adoration, no human words can reach out to the eternal glory of God, so that only astonished silence is left. Identity and difference are two complementary aspects in the counter-running movements of utterance and adoration.

2. The Cosmogony of Tao and God's Creation

According to Lao Tsu's book, all things proceed from the Tao, and return to the Tao. For 'all things' the expression 'the ten thousand things' is generally used. We shall look first at the ideas about the origin of the ten thousand things, and then at the Tao's workings in them.

The Tao itself is described through *non-being* and *being*, so the ten thousand things proceed from the being of the Tao, but this being proceeds from the non-being of the Tao:

> The ten thousand things are born of being.
> Being is born of not being.
>
> (Ch. 40)

The originating of all things out of the being of the Tao is thought of – as it is in the neo-Platonism of Plotinus – as being a triadic self-evolution of the Tao. In the famous Chapter 42 we read:

> The Tao [way] begot one.
> One begot two.
> Two begot three.
> And three begot the ten thousand things.

In popular Taoism, this primal threeness is imagined as 'the three pure ones'. These are the three heavenly Lords, who are sometimes pictured in a row behind one another, sometimes on a bench side by side. They are often linked with the three modes of time:

(a) Heavenly Lord: first original One, time past,
(b) Spiritual Lord: Jade-Imperial One, time present,
(c) Divine Lord: Pure Dawn One, time to come.

This is the way they can be seen in the White Cloud Daoist Temple in Peking. The verb 'create' is not an appropriate translation in the Taost context, because it introduces the biblical concept of creation found in the Genesis account. It is better to talk about 'coming into being', 'originating' and – actively – 'producing'. No difference is made between the triadic self-evolution of the 'being' side of the Tao and the emergence of the 'ten thousand things'; the same verb is used for both. This indicates that the Taoist theogony is carried forward in the cosmogony of the ten thousand things. But this continuation is not thought of as a continuous sequence: oneness – twoness – threeness symbolize heaven. In the West too, heaven is symbolized by the number three, the earth, in contrast to heaven, by the number four. The Temple of Heaven in Peking is surrounded by a circle of three steps, and is roofed with three curved roofs. The enclosure is then the quadrangle of the earth. The circle is the sign of perfection, because it is the image of the primal and endless eternity. '[Unendangered, it moves in a circle]', says Ch. 25 about the Tao. When the Tao develops itself and rounds itself out triadically to its perfection in heaven, heaven becomes 'the law of the earth'. Everything earthly lives in harmony with the Tao if it lives in harmony with heaven. So in this graduated self-evolution of the Tao human beings find '[the law of the earth]' (Ch. 25); and through this law they may be joined with heaven – through heaven with the triad of the Tao – through the triad of the Tao with the being of all being – and through the eternal being of Tao with the eternal not-being out of which the being of the Tao proceeds.

The symbol Taoism takes for the origin of the ten thousand things is not the male 'create'; it is the female 'bear' or 'give birth'.

> The beginning of the universe
> Is the mother of all things.
> Knowing the mother, one also knows the sons.
>
> (Ch. 52)

Chapter 25 says about the Tao itself:

> Perhaps it is the mother of ten thousand things.
> I do not know its name.
> Call it Tao [way].

The female symbolism for Tao and the earth is important, because this symbolism also marks the virtues of the way. The life-giving power sustains the living, but does not dominate it. It gives life, but then takes itself back, withdraws, so that the living can develop independently.

> [The ten thousand things emerge from the way,
> but the way claims no power.]
> Creating not possessing,
> [Helping] yet taking no credit.
> Work is done then forgotten.
> [Because it claims no merit, its merit] lasts forever.
>
> (Ch. 2)

The primal and female is often compared with a valley, which receives the streams and takes up the water. From it the ten thousand living things emerge and are nourished and sustained.

> The valley spirit never dies;
> It is the woman, primal mother.
> Her gateway is the root of heaven and earth.
> It is like a veil barely seen.
> [but it is always present.
> Use it, it is inexaustible].
>
> (Ch. 6)

The metaphor of the female and motherly for Tao does not merely take its life-bearing and life-nourishing power as analogy, but also the characteristics which a Confucian, patriarchal society ascribes to the humiliated woman. This is undoubtedly the subversive – even revolutionary – element in the *Tao Te Ching*. Men may make history, but women preserve nature. So in the long run it is not the men who are the victors; it is the women.

> The female overcomes the male with stillness,
> Lying low in stillness.
>
> (Ch. 61)

From this Lao Tsu develops some general wisdom. Stillness overcomes noise because it endures. The lower overcomes the higher, because it receives and gathers together. The weak conquers the strong, and the soft the hard.

> A man is born gentle and weak.
> At his death he is hard and stiff.
> [When the ten thousand things,
> When grasses and flowers grow],
> They are tender and filled with sap;
> At their death they are withered and dry.
> Therefore the stiff and unbending is the [companion] of death.
> The gentle and yielding is the [companion] of life.
> The hard and strong will fall.
> The soft and weak will overcome.
>
> (Ch. 76)

What is in the long term stronger, water or rock? Lao Tsu answers:

> Under heaven nothing is more soft and yielding than water.
> Yet for attacking the solid and strong, nothing is better;
> It has no equal.
> [The not-being makes it easy for it.]
>
> (Ch. 78)

For the political virtue which is in harmony with the cosmic Tao this means that the one who humiliates himself wins, and the one who takes upon himself the country's dirt, will become the country's king. This wisdom is paralleled only in Isaiah 53, in the Suffering Servant, and in the Christ hymn in chapter 2 of the Epistle to the Philippians.

> If a great country gives way to a smaller country,
> It will conquer the smaller country.
>
> (Ch. 61)

[He who takes upon himself the dirt in the land
Can be called the lord of the altar of the fields and the corn.]
He who takes upon himself the country's disasters
[is destined] to be the king of the [earth].

(Ch. 78)

This dialectic – through servitude to rule – was only taken up again in philosophy with Hegel. The book adds to it by saying:

The truth often sounds paradoxical.

But it only sounds paradoxical in a perverse, untrue world of injustice and violence directed against human beings and against the earth; and that also means against the Tao, which keeps human beings and the earth alive.

Among the metaphors for Tao drawn from nature, and in addition to female and motherly metaphors, Lao Tsu has a special liking for *water*, because running water gives life.

The highest good is like water.
Water gives life to the ten thousand things and does not strive.

(Ch. 8)

[If you will compare Tao's existence in the world,
 It is like the brook, the river in the valley.]
Tao in the world is like a river flowing home to the sea.

(Ch. 32)

Water is also the metaphor we find used in the Bible for the Spirit of life 'poured out on all flesh' so that it may be eternally living. 'All flesh' means all the living. The gentle power of the life-giving water finds its correspondence in the gentleness of the Taoist sage and the followers of Christ:

Blessed are the meek,
For they shall inherit the earth.

(Matt. 5.5)

If we now shift our perspective, and look away from the Taoist cosmogony to the biblical accounts of creation in Genesis 1 and 2, the differences leap to the eye. On the one hand we find a doctrine about the emergence of the world – on the other a doctrine about the world's creation; on the one hand a non-personal or supra-personal Tao – on the other a transcendent, personal Creator God; on the one hand a way – on the other hand a Word; on the one hand the 'ten thousand things' first of all, and then human beings too – on the other a creation for the sake of human beings; on the one hand the human being is to observe the law of the earth – on the other hand, as God's 'image', he is to 'subdue' the earth. We could go on, but it would not be particularly fruitful. Let us rather look at the correspondences and harmonizations, for this is the same reality: the reality which Tao teaches us to perceive, and the reality which belief in creation intends to reveal to us.

(a) The biblical story of creation teaches us to understand God's free creative work (Hebrew *barah*) as a creation which has no presuppositions; it is a *creatio ex nihilo*, as later terminology put it – a creation out of nothing. But where is this Nothing supposed to be, if the One God is omnipresent? For his presence then has no limits. So in fact there can be no *extra Deum*, nothing outside God. We find the only convincing explanation in the Kabbalah tradition, with its concept of *zimzum*: God restricts his omnipresence, withdraws himself, and by doing so concedes a space of absolute nothingness – that is to say, a space of God's non-being – into which he calls his creation 'out of non-being into being' (Rom 4.17). To put it in Taoistic terms, the Being of God the Creator and the existence of his creation then proceed out of the non-being God has conceded. Even without knowing the Kabbalah, John Scotus Erigena did not find ideas of this kind alien since, in neo-Platonic fashion, he saw the 'nothing' out of which God creates his creation as God himself: *creatio ex nihilo* is *creatio e Deo* – creation out of nothing is creation out of God, because God is both being and nothingness.

(b) The biblical doctrine of creation is not to be found only in the book of Genesis. We can discover it in Israel's Wisdom literature as well. Whereas the account of creation in the Priestly Writing stresses God's transcendence over against his creation, Wisdom teaching sees the indwelling of God in his creation by virtue of his Spirit (*ruach*) and his wisdom (*hokma*). Through his creative Word, God calls into being the things that are not; but through his wisdom he 'makes', forms and shapes all things, and holds them together in an ordered community. So, in Proverbs 8.22ff., the Wisdom of God says:

> The Lord created me at the beginning of his ways;
> Before he created anything I was there.
> I was set up from eternity,
> From the beginning, before the earth . . .
> When he established the heavens, I was there,
> When he drew a circle on the face of the deep . . .
> Then I was beside him like a master workman;
> And I was daily his delight, playing before him always,
> Playing in his inhabited world,
> And delighting in the sons of men.

The parallels to the description of Tao and the way it acts in the ten thousand things are striking. Here 'Wisdom' appears as the principle immanent in the creation of the creation-transcendent God. It stands more or less in the same place as the oneness – twoness – threeness, for it is already there when the heavens are prepared. But its way of acting in the world of the ten thousand things is described as childlike rather than motherly. It is not withdrawal and not-doing (*wuh-wei*) which becomes the world-symbol for Israel's Wisdom; it is *play*. For the Chinese Tao, *tzu-yan* is the highest reality of not-doing (*wuh-wei*). What is meant is nothing other than matter-of-course spontaneity, and this corresponds precisely to the self-forgetting, delighted play of Wisdom on the earth and among human beings.

'Eternally the woman with her stillness overcomes the male' says Lao Tsu. But 'unless you become like children, you will never enter the kingdom of God', said Jesus. Through its spontaneity the child has the advantage over the male and the female. The messianism of the child leaves the hard patriarchy and the soft matriarchy behind, and embodies the hope for the future of the liberated life. Because of that, although in Israel's book of Proverbs Wisdom is presented as 'Lady Wisdom', she is described as a child playing with delight and love. With every child new life begins.

(c) Christian theological tradition ascribes not only the creation of the world to God's omnipotence, but its preservation from its annihilation too. God is the owner and Lord of his world. He can do with it what he likes. Consequently all the events of world history, and the events in our own world too, must be accepted from the hand of his Providence, even if we do not understand it. But it is one-sided to rest the preservation of creation on God's omnipotence, if by omnipotence we mean merely super-power, and if we understand by God's freedom only his freedom of choice, or even his caprice. The Orthodox theology of the eastern churches has always understood God's almighty power rather as his patience. God preserves this world in spite of its inner contradictions and the threat of its self-annihilation, through his *long-suffering* and his *patience*. It is because of his patience that 'we are not quite cut off' (Lam. 3.22). But patience is nothing other than *the capacity for suffering* and the readiness to suffer, on the foundation of hope: 'Patience is the art of hope.' Because God hopes for the return of human beings and the homecoming of his creation, he sustains creation with unending patience, allows it time and gives it space for freedom. The fact that God does not intervene from above with lightning and thunder when evil is rampant is not a sign of his absence; it is a sign of the presence of his hoping patience. God suffers the contradiction of the act of violence, and the earth's blood cries out to high heaven. But his patience, his stillness and his weakness, to use Lao Tsu's language, are 'the companion of life' and will overcome the rigid and the strong which are 'the companions of death'.

God's activity in sustaining creation and preserving it can very well be described in the Christian sense with characteristics of the Tao. And the conviction that ultimately the winner is the one

who humbles himself and carries the dirt of the earth is closer to
the wisdom of the suffering Servant of God in the Old and New
Testament than anything else in the history of religion. 'He who
takes upon himself the country's disaster is destined to be the
king of the earth': that could be written in the Christian book
too. It discloses to Christians afresh the truth of the suffering and
crucified Christ whom they call Lord. The lords of this world
come and go, but the One who bears the suffering of the world
and the sins of the world remains eternally, and to him is due
honour and glory and blessing to all eternity (Rev. 5.12).

3. The Return of the Tao and Enlightenment: What is Deliverance?

Just as the ten thousand things proceed from the Tao, so they
return to Tao again and, together with them, the Tao returns to
itself. All things move from Tao to Tao in the great cycle of the
Tao.

> [All things emerge together
> And I see them return again.]
> They grow and flourish and then return to the source.
> Returning to the source is stillness.
> [Stillness means returning to what is destined.]
> Returning to what is destined means to be [enlightened].
> To know the eternal means enlightenment.
>
> (Ch. 16)

All things return to the Tao, just as they have emerged from the
Tao: that is their deliverance. They return to the ground in which
they are rooted, where they come to rest and remain eternally. In
this homecoming the things find the way to that for which they
were destined. That is the meaning of their existence and the goal
of their movement. This emergence and return determines the
cycle of nature on this earth: day and night, summer and winter,
springtime and the fall of the year. For Lao Tsu this idea of the

cycle, of circulation, is so powerful that he also uses it for the metaphysics of the world. There, the Tao is not merely origin and goal, but is itself the movement: the Tao issues out of itself into the ten thousand things, and together with them returns to itself. 'Returning is the motion of the Tao.' '[The movement of the Tao (way) is contrary]' (Ch. 40). Where does the Tao return to? It ultimately returns to its nothingness. 'It returns to nothingness.' 'It has found the way home to what is without being' (Ch. 14). The return of the Tao to itself secures for all being the corresponding return to their foundation. In harmony with the Tao, they return home.

It is important that at this point Lao Tsu should talk about the 'enlightenment' of the wise man. Tracing back the sequence of ideas from their end: enlightenment means to know the eternal; to know the eternal means to know what is destined; to know what is destined means to find rest and be still. It is in this that 'harmony' with the Tao is to be found (Ch. 55). It is in this that desire ends. 'Ever desireless, one can see the mystery [of the Tao/way]' (Ch. 1). Here (wilful) acting ends. 'Less and less is done until non-action (*wuh-wei*) is achieved. When nothing is done, nothing is left undone' (Ch. 48). ['Eternally it happens of itself'] (Ch. 51).

> Creating without claiming,
> Doing without taking credit,
> Guiding without interfering –
> This is Primal [mystical] Virtue.
>   (Ch. 51)

The idea of the return has deeply moulded Christian metaphysics too, from Thomas Aquinas to Hegel. Everything comes from God – everything goes to God. To the *exitus* of all things from God the *reditus* of all things to God corresponds. The goal is the counter-image to the origin. The end is like the beginning. The movement of the world is a single great cycle or circulation. All linear movements in the world are merely segments of the world's great circular movement. The many proceed from the

One, and the many return to the One. The movement of the return to God is the movement of salvation. Without the return to the origin there is no salvation. And salvation is that all moved things should come to 'rest' in their origin in God.

But what drives the things forward, away from their eternal origin in God, and what leads them back to it? It is God's creative Spirit which brings them forth, and it is God's redeeming Spirit which brings them back again. For Hegel, this world-process out of God and to God is the process of the self-fulfilment of the Absolute Spirit, which comes to itself by going out of itself. We interpreted the triad oneness – twoness – threeness (according to Ch. 42) as the 'self-evolving process' of the Tao; and the process of the return of all things is then in harmony with the process of self-fulfilment in which the Tao comes to itself. But that is perhaps only to see the return process of the Tao through western eyes.

In the Christian idea of world history, the beginning and the end do not correspond, for the end is greater than the beginning. It begins with creation in time, and ends in the eternal kingdom of God. Everything that happens in history between creation and kingdom is transformed through the final Judgement, and is caught up and brought into God's eternal kingdom. So although there is a correspondence between end and beginning, there is not an identity. The time created with the creation of all things does not have a circular structure, but is determined by the transcendence of the future of the eternal kingdom. It follows that the creation in time has to be understood not as a 'closed system', with a circular temporal structure, but as an 'open system', with an irreversible temporal structure. The world of Tao, however, is a kind of 'closed system', with a circular temporal structure. The emergence and return of the ten thousand things can be unremittingly repeated, but the movement is always the same. The world of Tao is not open for the future. The virtue of the way, *Te*, does not point towards the future. 'Enlightenment' is in harmony with the eternal Tao – not so hope, which according to the biblical concept runs ahead, in harmony with God's promise.

4. The Life of the World: Ch'i and Ruach

Ideas about the divine power of life in the *Tao te Ching* and in the Old Testament are particularly close to each other. What is termed *Ch'i* in the one and *ruach* in the other are similar in more than one respect. And yet the differences are patent.

Lao Tsu uses the old Chinese term *Ch'i* as a name for that which gives life, keeps life in harmonious movement, and preserves life. He also calls it 'oneness'.

[From ancient times many things achieved oneness:
Thanks to the oneness the sky is clear,
Thanks to the oneness the earth is firm,
Thanks to the oneness the gods are mighty,
Thanks to the oneness the valley is fruitful,
Thanks to the oneness kings and princes are the model for the
    world.
All this is through the virtue of oneness.
Without that which makes the ten thousand things live
They would perish.]

(Ch. 39)

According to Chapter 42, 'oneness' is the first thing which Tao begets. The 'twoness' and the 'threeness' follow from it.

Three begot the ten thousand things.
The ten thousand things carry Yin and embrace Yang.
They achieve harmony by combining these forces.

(Ch. 42)

Yin is the resting Yin-Ch'i and Yang is the moving Yang Ch'i, so 'oneness' means the Ch'i itself, and Yin-Ch'i and Yang-Ch'i mean the complementary forces of Ch'i which keep all the transitions from rest into movement and from movement into rest in 'harmony' with the Tao. 'Harmony' always means correspondence with the Tao. What originally proceeds from the being of the Tao as the first thing is the life of Ch'i. It is the power of life and the space for living, the time of life and the relationships of life in one.

According to ancient Chinese philosophy, the Ch'i is the omnipresent, formless but all-forming power of existence, of all the living and of human beings too. Because it is formless, it can form everything. Because it is empty, it can take in all things. Because it is the 'between' of all things, it can bring about the universal sympathy of living beings. So Chapter 42 says about the complementary forces Yin and Yang:

[The breath of emptiness makes their harmony.]

Yin and Yang are not meant in the sense of two different forces. They are the complementary transitions and rhythms of nature: cold and heat, light and darkness, coming into being and passing away, birth and death, and so forth. If Yin and Yang do not harmonize, cold and heat do not come at the proper time. When they interpenetrate each other, all living things are the result. So this is not a unified principle of complementarity. It does not come into being between things. The things emerge and acquire form from the complementary movements. This does not apply only to partial processes, such as day and night, light and darkness. It is true of the whole of nature's life, human beings included. All beings, movements and changes in the world are involved in a great sympathy, says Chuang Tse. 'Everthing is eternally inwardly related', as the German Romantic poet Clemens von Brentano wrote. Ch'i is a kind of world-spirit, which quickens, moves, changes and secures everything. In it, the ten thousand things rely on each other and are dependent on each other.

In the Old Testament God's *ruach* is described in a very similar way. Before God creates 'the ten thousand things' through his Word, the *ruach* is present, hovering above chaos with its vibrating field of energy (Gen. 1.2). The word *ruach* is onomatopoeic, echoing the tempest, like Ch'i, but it means both the breath of the eternal God and the vitality of created beings.

Psalm 104. 29f. writes:

When thou takest away their breath (vitality, spirit of life),
    they die,
When thou sendest forth thy Spirit (vitality and divine energy)
    they are created;
And thou renewest the face of the earth.

Job 34.14 puts it in a very similar way:

If he (God) should take back his *ruach* and his breath to
    himself,
All flesh would perish together,
And man would return to dust.

God the Creator is a 'friend of life', says Wisdom 11.26.
Consequently his 'imperishable spirit is in all things'.

These few quotations from the Old Testament make it clear
that living things are created from the continual flow of *ruach*.
They exist in the power of *ruach* and are renewed out of it. It is
God's *ruach* which brings about the existence, the form and the
transformations of all created beings. It holds together the community of creation in the mutual exchange of life. The divine
ruach is nothing less than 'the cosmic spirit'. The orders and
transformations of creation manifest the wisdom of God, which
is often identified with God's *ruach*. 'The Spirit of the Lord fills
the world' (Wis. 1.7).

Since, according to the biblical view, all things are created
through the Word, they can also be differentiated from one
another by name. They are not fleeting phenomena on the cosmic
fields of energy. But because they are all created in the same
Spirit, they belong together in a great, harmonious community.
Creation through the Word and mediation through the Spirit are
as complementary as are wave and particle in modern nuclear
physics. In contrast to this, Taoistic thinking seems to prefer the
energy fields of Yin and Yan. The 'Book of Transformations',
I Ching, shows this. The emphases are different from those in
'the book of creation'.

In talking about the *ruach,* the Bible makes a fine differentiation. There is God's *ruach,* and there is the *ruach* of created beings, while the New Testament talks about God's *pneuma* and our *pneuma* (Rom. 8.15). This distinction in the Spirit firmly establishes the qualitative difference between God the Creator and those he has created. The life-spirit of the world comes from the eternal Spirit of God, but the two are not identical. The eternal Spirit of God is a divine subject, but the life-spirit of the world is an impersonal medium which interpenetrates everything and lives in all the living. This differentiation cannot be found in the *Tao Te Ching.* Ch'i is the First to proceed from the being of the Tao, and it is at the same time that which interpenetrates, orders and changes everything. It is not merely divine; it is even more than divine, because the gods are powerful only 'thanks to the One'.

The Chinese book of wisdom is very close to the Jewish and Christian book of wisdom, and very remote from it. The closer it comes to us, the more we recognize the differences. The more we perceive the differences, the better we understand it. Common to both wisdoms is the mysterious nature with which we seek to find a harmony through the way we live.

Notes

I Theology in the World of the Modern Sciences

1. Since this essay was published, the discussion has moved on. From the relevant literature, I may point to the following works: A. Peacocke, *Creation and the World of Science*, Oxford, 1979; T. Torrance, *Divine and Contingent Order*, Oxford, 1981; H. Rolston, *Science and Religion. A Critical Survey*, New York, 1987; W. Pannenberg, *Theology and the Philosophy of Science*, trans. F. McDonagh, London and Philadelphia, 1976; J. Polkinghorne, *One World. The Interaction of Science and Theology*, Princeton, 1987; I. Barbour, *Religion in an Age of Science*, San Francisco, 1990; Nancy Murphy, *Theology in an Age of Scientific Reasoning*, New York, 1990. However, my first contribution to the discussion between theology and science is perhaps not obsolete, but still has relevance, at least as my contribution to that discussion.

I was indebted in the original essay to the following studies: H. Gollwitzer, 'Die Theologie im Hause der Wissenschaften', *EvTh* 18, 1958, 14ff.; E. Wolf, 'Theologie und Naturwissenschaft', *MPTh* 54, 1965, 321ff.; Günter Howe, *Mensch und Physik*, Stuttgart, 1963; G. Picht, 'Naturwissenschaft und Bildung' in C. Münster and G. Picht, *Naturwissenschaft und Bildung* in *Weltbild und Erzeihung* 3, ed. F. Messerschmid *et al.*, 1953, 33ff.; G. Picht, 'Was heisst Aufklärung?', *Frankfurter Hefte* 19, 1964, 503ff.; G. Gloege, 'Der Mensch zwischen Naturwissenschaft und Theologie' in *Heilsgeschehen und Welt* I, Göttingen, 1965, 264ff.; C. J. Dippel and M. de Jong, *Geloof en Naturwetenschap* I, Amsterdam, 1965 (these are studies made from 1951 onwards, under the auspices of the Commission for Church and Theology of the Dutch Reformed Church).

2. Cf. W. Elert, *Morphologie des Luthertums* I, Munich, 1931 (reprint 1952), 363ff., and E. Hirsch, *Geschichte der neueren evangelischen Theologie* I, Gütersloh 1949, 115f. What Hirsch says must however be qualified, inasmuch as the term 'hypothesis' is taken from humanist rhetoric; it is only today that it has come to be interpreted in the sense of the scientific hypothesis. For the dispute between Copernicus and Osiander

about the preface, see the account in H. Blumenberg, *Die kopernikanische Wende*, Frankfurt, 1965, 92ff.

3. E. Hirsch, *Geschichte der ... evangelischen Theologie* I, 205.

4. Cf. here G. Krüger, *Freiheit und Weltverwaltung*, Freiburg, 1958, esp. 71ff. and 213ff.

5. B. Brecht, *Leben des Galilei*, 1962, preface; quoted in E. Wolf, 'Theologie und Naturwissenschaft', 322.

6. B. Pascal, *Oeuvres* II, 133, quoted in J. Pieper, *Über den Begriff der Tradition*, Freiburg, 1958, 10.

7. B. Pascal, *Pensées*, trans. J. M. Cohen (Harmondsworth, 1961), 222: 'The God of the Christians is not simply a God who is the author of mathematical truths and of the order of the elements; that is the view of the heathen and of the Epicureans ... But the God of Abraham, the God of Isaac, the God of Jacob, the God of the Christians, is a God of love and consolation; He is a God who fills the soul and the heart of those whom He possesses; He is a God who gives them an inner consciousness of their misery and of His infinite mercy ... What meets our eyes denotes neither a total absence nor a manifest presence of the divine, but the presence of a God who conceals himself. Everything bears this stamp.'

8. R. Descartes, *Meditations*, Preface to the Reader in *Discourse on Method*, trans. J. Veitch, London and New York, 1912.

9. K. Marx, *Die Frühschriften*, ed. S. Landshut, Stuttgart, 1953, reprint 1964, 330.

10. F. Baader, quoted in G. Howe, *Mensch und Physik*, 120. Cf. also his insight into the dialectical interrelation of faith and knowledge, *Über die Zwiespalt des religiösen Glaubens und Wissens*, second ed., Darmstadt, 1958, 49: 'As we know, this conflict is both historical and as if its nature was related to the conflict between faith and efficacy, in that the efficacy stripped of faith is not the proper efficacy, and that faith stripped of efficacy not the true faith, as if the knowledge stripped of faith was not true knowledge, and the faith stripped of knowledge not the proper, true faith.'

11. F. Schleiermacher, 'Sendschreiben an Dr. Lücke', as introduction to *Der Christliche Glaube nach den Grundsätzen der evangelischen Kirche*, as quoted in Bibliothek theologischer Klassiker, vol. 13, Gottha, 1889, 36 (not included in the ET *The Christian Faith*).

12. R. Bultmann, 'The Understanding of Man and the World in the New Testament and in the Greek World' in *Essays Philosophical and Theological* (ET of selections from his *Glauben und Verstehen*), London and New York, 1955, 88.

13. K. Barth, *CD* III/1, Preface, x (trans. slightly altered). On both Barth and Bultmann in this connection, cf. G. Altner, *Schöpfungsglaube und Entwicklungsgedanke in der protestantischen Theologie zwischen E. Haeckel und Teilhard de Chardin*, Zürich, 1965, 84ff.

14. C.F. von Weizsäcker, *Zum Weltbild der Physik*, seventh ed., Zürich, 1958, 263.

15. J. Ritter, *Hegel und die französische Revolution*, Cologne, Opladen, 1957, 33; G. Rohrmoser, *Subjektivität und Verdinglichung. Theologie und Gesellschaft im Denken des jungen Hegel*, Frankfurt, 1961.

16. H. U. von Balthasar, *Die Gottesfrage des heutigen Menschen*, Vienna and Munich, 1956, 52.

17. Cf. G. Ebeling, 'Theologie', RGG³ VI, col. 754ff.

18. F. Nietzsche, *Die fröhliche Wissenschaft*, no. 125 in *Werke*, ed. F. Schlechta, vol. 2, Munich, 1955, 127. (Cf. *The Joyful Wisdom*, trans. T. Common, *Complete Works of F. Nietzsche* X, 1910, 168. The present quotation has been translated directly from the German.)

19. G. W. F. Hegel, *Faith and Knowledge*, trans. W. Cerf and H. S. Harris, Albany, NY, 1977, in Peter C. Hodgson, *Hegel. Theologian of the Spirit*, Minneapolis, 1997, 73.

20. I. Kant, *Critique of Pure Reason*, trans. and ed. N. Kemp Smith, London, 1929, revised 1933, *Preface* to the second ed., 20. Cf. also the interpretation in G. Picht, 'Naturwissenschaft und Bildung', 105ff., which I am following here.

21. Similarly W. Heisenberg, quoted in G. Howe, *Mensch und Physik*, 74.

22. H. Weyl, quoted in G. Howe, *Mensch und Physik*, 53.

23. W. Heisenberg, quoted in G. Howe, *Mensch und Physik*, 74.

24. H. Hensel in *Studium generale* 15, 1962, 747.

25. V. E. von Gebsattel, *Prolegomena einer medizinischen Anthropologie* IV, Berlin, 1954.

26. Cf. here H. Thomae, 'Psychologie' in *Wege zu einer pädagogischen Anthropologie*, Pädagogische Forschungen 23, ed. A. Flitner, Heidelberg, 1963, 92.

27. G. Picht, 'Naturwissenschaft und Bildung', 115.

28. G. W. F. Hegel, Preface to the *Phenomenology of Spirit*, trans. J. Michael Stewart in *Hegel. Theologian of the Spirit*, 94.

29. Ernst Bloch called the open world process a *laboratorium possibilis salutis* (a laboratory of possible salvation). Cf. *Tübinger Einleitung in die Philosophie*, Frankfurt, 1970, 217. Also E. Bloch, *Das Prinzip Hoffnung*, Frankfurt, 1959, 225–35 (*The Principle of Hope*, trans. N. and S. Plaice and P. Knight, Cambridge, Mass., and Oxford, 1986).

30. L. Landgrebe, 'Das philosophische Problem des Endes der Geschichte' in *Phänomenologie und Geschichte*, Gütersloh, 1967.

31. H. Gollwitzer, 'Theologie im Hause der Wissenschaften', 33.

32. J. Moltmann, *Theology of Hope*, trans. J. W. Leitch, London and New York, 1967, latest reprint, London, 2002.

33. This has been shown in an illuminating way by L. Landgrebe in 'Das philosophische Problem des Endes der Geschichte', on the basis of Kant's writing *Das Ende aller Dinge* and E. Husserl's concept of time.

34. I am taking over this expression from H. G. Gadamer, *Wahrheit und Methode*, Tübingen, 1960, second ed. 1965, 288 (see *Truth and Method*, trans. and ed. G. Barden and J. Cumming, second corrected ed., London and New York, 1979).

35. L. Landgrebe, 'Das philosophische Problem des Endes der Geschichte'.

36. N. M. Wildiers, *Teilhard de Chardin*, Paris, 1960; also S. Daecke, 'Bericht über die Teilhard de Chardin-Literatur', *MPTh* 55, 1966, 257–69 and 312–28.

37. C. J. Dippel and G. de Santillana, quoted in E. Wolf, 'Theologie und Naturwissenschaft', 331.

38. G. Picht, 'Was heisst Aufklärung?', *Frankfurter Hefte*, 1964, 506.

39. Cf. H. Kipphardt's stylized 'scenic report', *In der Sache J. Robert Oppenheimer*, Frankfurt, 1965.

40. E. Wolf, 'Theologie und Naturwissenschaft', 332.

41. G. Howe, *Mensch und Physik*, 117ff.

42. M. Weber, 'Wissenschaft als Beruf (1919), fifth ed. 1967, 37; also in *Gesammelte Aufsätze zur Wissenschaftslehre*, 1922, 555. (Trans. by H. H. Gerth and C. Wright Mills in *From Max Weber: Essays in Sociology* [London 1948; new ed. 1998]. The present passage has been translated directly from the German.)

II *Theologians and Scientists on the Way to Wisdom*

1. What seem to me successful attempts can be found in E. von Weizsäcker, *Offene Systeme I, Beiträge zur Zeitstruktur, Entropie und Evolution*, Stuttgart, 1974, and in J. Polkinghorne and M. Welker (eds), *The End of the World and the Ends of God. Science and Theology on Eschatology*, Harrisburg, PA, 2000. For a good survey, see M. Welker, 'Springing Cultural Traps: The Science-and-Theology Discourse on Eschatology and the Common Good', *Theology Today* 58/2, July 2001, 165–76.

2. Thomas F. Torrance is a notable exception. Cf. his books *Christian Theology and Scientific Culture*, Belfast, 1980, and *Divine und Contingent Order*, Oxford, 1981. He was awarded the Templeton Prize in 1978.

3. Michael Polanyi must be mentioned here; see his book *The Tacit Dimension*, New York, 1966.

4. G. Altner (ed.), *Menschenwürde und biotechnischer Fortschritt im Horizont theologischer und sozialethischer Erwägungen*, special number *EvTh* 61, Gütersloh, 2001, with contributions by G. Altner, K. Dörner, R. Kollek, D. Mieth, E. Pelkner, D. von der Pfordten, I. Praetorius and U. Theile.

5. M. Horkheimer, *Critical Theory*, trans. M.J. O'Connell *et al.*, New

York, 1972; M. Horkheimer, *Critique of Instrumental Reason*, trans. M. J. O'Connell *et al.*, New York, 1974.

6. See Celia Deane-Drummond's excellent book, *Creation through Wisdom. Theology and the New Biology*, Edinburgh, 2000.

7. This was rightly pointed out by John Paul II in his encyclical *Fides et Ratio* (1998): wisdom is able to overcome the gap between faith and reason.

8. This was also Ernst Bloch's vision of harmonization with the still hidden 'subject nature'. See *Das Prinzip Hoffnung*, Frankfurt, 1959, § 37 II, 802–13 (*The Principle of Hope*, trans. N. and S. Plaice and P. Knight, Cambridge, Mass., and Oxford, 1986).

III Creation as an Open System

1. Cf. A. Koyré, *From the Closed World to the Infinite Universe*, Baltimore, 1957, 1968.

2. F. Gogarten and R. Bultmann inclined to these solutions. For a critical view, cf. C. J. Dippel and J. M. de Jong, *Geloof en Naturwetenshap*, Part 1, The Hague, 1965.

3. Cf. K. Barth, *CD* III/1, Preface. But as the anthropology he develops in this volume shows, he himself did not adhere to this peaceful division between theology and science. On this point cf. C. Link, *Die Welt als Gleichnis. Studien zum Problem der natürlichen Theologie*, Munich, 1976.

4. In his orientation towards an eschatological doctrine of creation I agree with W. Pannenberg. See his books *Towards a Theory of Nature – essays on science and faith*, ed. T. Peters, Louisville, KY, 1993) and *Theology and the Kingdom of God*, Philadelphia, 1969 (first published in English). But his representation of the Being of God as 'the power of the future', which is in accord with the 'theology of hope', is in my view one-sided, because it overlooks the power of God's suffering. Cf. my book *The Crucified God*, trans. R. A. Wilson and J. Bowden, London, 1974.

5. M. Eliade, *The Myth of the Eternal Return*, trans. from French by W. R. Trask, New York, 1954, London, 1955; W. F. Otto, *Die Gestalt und das Sein*, Munich, 1955; E. Hornung, *Die Geschichte als Fest*, Darmstadt, 1966.

6. 'Finis rerum respondet principio, Deus enim principium et finis rerum. Ergo et exitus rerum a principio respondet reductioni rerum in finem?' (Thomas Aquinas, *STh* 1a 90.3 [Latin text with English translation], vol. 13, Blackfriars, London and New York, 1964).

7. 'In exitu creaturarum a primo principio attenditur quaedam circulatio vel regiratio, eo quod omnia revertuntur sicut in finem in id, a quo sicut principio prodierunt. Et ideo oportet ut per eadem quibus est exitus in principio, et reditus in finem attendatur' (I. *Sent.* d. 14, q 2 a 2). On Aquinas's view, see the comment by M. Seckler, *Das Heil in der Geschichte*.

Geschichtstheologisches Denken bei Thomas vom Aquin, Munich, 1964.

8. R. Bultmann, 'The Concept of Revelation in the New Testament' (1929) in S. M. Ogden (ed.), *Existence and Faith. Shorter Writings of R. Bultmann*, London, 1961, 58–91.

9. G. von Rad, *Old Testament Theology* I, trans. D. M. G. Stalker, Edinburgh and London, 1962, reissued 1975, 136ff.; quotation on 138 [trans. slightly altered]. W. H. Schmidt, *Die Schöpfungsgeschichte*, Neukirchen, 1967. There has been a more recent attempt in Old Testament research to find an approach to belief in creation no longer by way of 'salvation history' but also by way of 'Wisdom'. Cf. G. von Rad, *Wisdom in Israel*, trans. J. D. Martin, London and Nashville, 1972; H. H. Schmid, 'Schöpfung, Gerechtigkeit und Heil. "Schöpfungstheologie" als Gesamthorizont biblischer Theologie', *ZThK* 10, 1973, 1–19; C. Westermann, *Genesis 1–11. A Commentary*, trans. J. J. Scullion, Minneapolis and London, 1984; G. Liedke, 'Selbstoffenbarung der Schöpfung', *EvKomm* 7, 1975, 298–400. I understand this approach as a supplement rather than as an alternative to the salvation-history approach to belief in creation.

10. G. von Rad, *Old Testament Theology* I, 139.

11. L. Köhler, *Old Testament Theology*, ET of third ed., London, 1957, Philadelphia, 1958, 88.

12. H. D. Preuss, *Jahweglaube und Zukunftshoffnung*, Stuttgart, 1968, 97f.

13. L. Köhler, *Old Testament Theology*, 143.

14. On necessity, chance and pleasure in the theory of play, cf. J. Moltmann, *Theology of Play*, ET New York, 1972 [*Theology and Joy*, London, 1973].

15. The openness of a system means: (1) that the system has different possibilities of alteration; (2) that its future behaviour has not been totally determined by its previous behaviour; (3) that it is communicable for other systems; and (4) that the final condition of the system is different from its initial state. Viewed scientifically, the 'closed system' is only a hypothesis, set up so that we may arrive at statements that can be quantified. In itself there is no such thing as a 'closed system'; at least, no statements can be made about closed systems, because they elude all observation. Statements can only be made about open systems, with which an exchange of information is possible. Every exchange of information needs carriers, in terms of material or energy. But a closed system would by definition be a system which had no exchange of material with the environment. Cf. E. von Weizsäcker (ed.), *Offene Systeme I. Beiträge zur Zeitstruktur von Information, Entropie und Evolution*, Stuttgart, 1974; H. Wehrt, 'Über Zeitverständnisse und die Problematik von Möglichkeit und Offenheit' in A. M. K. Müller (ed.), *Zukunftsperspektiven zu einem integrierten*

Verständnis der Lebenswelt, Stuttgart, 1976, 144–208, in relation to the 'theology of hope'.

16. Cf. W. Pannenberg, *Theology and the Kingdom of God*, 78f.

17. Cf. J. Moltmann, *The Crucified God*, 267ff.

18. H. Schwantes, *Schöpfung der Endzeit*, Stuttgart, 1962.

19. E. Käsemann, 'Primitive Christian Apocalyptic' in *New Testament Questions of Today*, trans. W. J. Montague, London, 1969, 132ff. My expression 'the concept of *aparch*' is intended to bring out the positive aspect of what Käsemann calls the 'eschatologische Vorbehalt' – the eschatological proviso. What is meant is thinking in terms of a beginning, not of an ending.

20. Contrary to E. Brunner, *Eternal Hope*, trans. H. Knight, London, 1954, 198ff., esp. 203: 'The negative point is sharp and definite – that "the form of this world passeth away, that death and transience will no longer be". But, apart from what directly concerns the new life of man and humanity, the positive side is left almost completely vague.' Cf. also J. B. Metz, *Theology of the World*, trans. W. Glenn-Doepel, London and New York, 1969, 97: 'Christian eschatology is not an omniscient ideology about the future, but a *theologia negativa* of the future.' But Metz sees the positive bond between present and future in love for 'the least of our brothers'.

21. Cf. G. Liedke, 'Von der Ausbeutung zur Kooperation. Theologisch-philosophische Überlegungen zum Problem des Umweltschutzes' in E. von Weizsäcker (ed.), *Humanökologie und Umweltschutz*, Stuttgart, 1972, 36–65. See also S. Bergmann, *Geist der Natur befreit. Die trinitarische Kosmologie Gregors von Nyssa im Horizont einer ökologischen Theologie der Befreiung*, Mainz, 1995.

22. W. Heisenberg, *The Physicist's Conception of Nature*, trans. A. J. Pomerans, New York and London, 1958, 29; similarly C. F. von Weizsäcker, *Die Einheit der Natur*, Munich, 1971, 279ff.

23. K. Marx, *Frühschriften,* ed. S. Landshut, Stuttgart, 1953, 237. But in *Capital* he is resignedly pessimistic about the achievability of a unity of being between man and nature. Cf. A. Schmidt, *Der Begriff der Natur in der Lehre von Marx*, second ed., Vienna, 1971; E. Roeder von Diersburg, *Zur Ontologie und Logik offener Systeme – Ernst Bloch vor dem Gesetz der Tradition*, Berlin, 1967.

24. The Bucharest Consultation of the World Council of Churches on Science and Technology for Human Development, June 1974; see *Anticipation* 18, August 1974, published by the Department on Church and Society of the WCC, Geneva.

25. C. Deane-Drummond, *Creation through Wisdom*, Edinburgh, 2000, see 138, 192 and 177.

IV God's Self-Restriction and the History of the Universe

1. For my attempt at a doctrine of creation which is compatible with the natural sciences, see *God in Creation. An ecological doctrine of creation* (the Gifford Lectures 1984–85), trans. Margaret Kohl, London and San Francisco, 1985. The present essay is an expanded version of a lecture held at the symposium of the John Templeton Foundation in Cambridge on 1 October 1998.

2. For the exegetical questions I should like to point to the excellent study by O. Hofius, *Der Christushymnus Phil 2,6–11. Untersuchungen zur Gestalt und Aussage eines urchristlichen Psalms*, Tübingen, 1976, and to R. Bauckham, *God Crucified. Monotheism and Christology in the New Testament*, Grand Rapids and Cambridge, 1998.

3. I should like to recommend here P. Althaus's article 'Kenosis' in RGG³ III, 1244–6, which is brief but very informative.

4. H. Urs von Balthasar, 'Mysterium Paschale' in *Mysterium Salutis* III/2, Einsiedlen, 1969, 133–326; also *Mysterium Paschale*, trans. with intro. by Aidan Nichols OP, Edinburgh, 1990, I should also like to point to the fruitfulness of the *kenosis* idea in the Christian-Buddhist dialogue; see J. Cobb Jr., (ed.), *The Emptying God. A Buddhist-Jewish-Christian Conversation*, New York, 1990. My dialogue with Masao Abe may also be found in this volume.

5. I have described the transformation of the metaphysically determined attribute of *immutabilis Dei* (God's unchangeableness) into the biblically based idea of the faithfulness of God in my book *Theology of Hope*, trans. J. W. Leitch, London, 1967, and the transformation of the metaphysically determined attribute of the *impassibilitas Dei* (God's inability to suffer) into the passibility of love in *The Crucified God*, trans. R. A. Wilson and J. Bowden, London, 1974. Schleiermacher, on the other hand, refused to ascribe to God 'a state of feeling especially excited by the suffering of others transformed into assistance'. He therefore excluded the concept of the mercy of God from Christian doctrine, assigning it to homiletic, practical and poetic ways of illustration: 'To attribute mercy to God is more appropriate to the language of poetry than to that of dogmatic thinking . . .' See *The Christian Faith*, ET of second ed., Edinburgh 1928, reprinted 1999, §85, Appendix: The Mercy of God, 353–4. To this Karl Barth responded: 'The source of the feeling of sheer dependence has no heart. But the personal God has a heart. He can feel, and be affected. He is not impassible' (*CD* II/1 370). If God cannot suffer he cannot have compassion either. The impassible God is the merciless God. If God cannot suffer, he cannot learn either. A God incapable of suffering is a foolish God.

6. The standard work is A. M. Goldberg, *Untersuchungen über die Vorstellung von der Schechinah in der frühen rabbinischen Literatur*, Berlin, 1969.

7. B. Janowski, '"Ich will in euerer Mitte wohnen." Struktur und Genese der exilischen *Shekina*-Theologie' in *Gottes Gegenwart in Israel. Beiträge zur Theologie des Alten Testaments*, Neukirchen, 1993, 119–47.

8. P. Kuhn, *Gottes Selbsterniedrigung in der Theologie der Rabbinen*, Munich, 1968. God carries Israel with its guilt 'like a servant' (84).

9. A. J. Heschel, *The Prophets*, New York, 1962, ch. 12: The Theology of Pathos, 221–67.

10. F. Rosenzweig, *Der Stern der Erlösung*, third ed., Heidelberg, 1954, III/3, 192–4 [*The Star of Redemption*, trans. W. W. Hallo, London, 1971]. The quotation has been translated directly from the German.

11. Luther's thought is echoed almost exactly in a poem by the seventeenth-century English poet Thomas Pestell:

> Hark, hark, the wise eternal Word
> Like a weak infant cries!
> In form of servant is the Lord.
> And God in cradle lies
> ('Behold the great Creator makes/ himself a house of clay').

12. W. H. Vanstone, *Love's Endeavour, Love's Expense. The Response of Being to the Love of God*, London, 1977, 120.

13. K. Barth, *CD* III /1, §42, 330ff.

14. G. Scholem, 'Schöpfung aus Nichts und Selbsverschränkung Gottes', *Eranos Jahrbuch* 25, 1956.

15. For more detail see J. Moltmann, *God in Creation*, Ch. VI: The Space of Creation, 140–57, esp. 153–7.

16. G. Scholem, *Major Trends in Jewish Mysticism*, New York, 1954, London, 1955, 244ff.

17. E. Brunner, *Dogmatics*, trans. O. Wyon, London, 1952, vol. II, 20: 'This, however, means that God does not wish to occupy the space of Being Himself, but that He wills to make room for other forms of existence. In so doing He limits Himself . . . The *kenosis* which reaches its climax in the cross of Christ already begins with the creation of the world' [trans. altered].

18. H. Jonas, *Zwischen Nichts und Ewigkeit. Zur Lehre vom Menschen*, Göttingen, 1963, 55–62 (with reference to the doctrine of evolution); F. Stern and H. Jonas, *Reflexionen finsterer Zeit*, Tübingen, 1984, 63–86: Der Gottesbegriff nach Auschwitz: 'So that the world might exist, and might exist for itself, God renounced his own being; he divested himself of his divinity in order to receive it again from the odyssey of time, laden with the fortuitous harvest of unforeseeable temporal experience, transfigured or perhaps also *distorted by them* . . . Only with the creation out of nothing do we have the *unity* of the divine principle together with its *self*-restriction, which gives *space* for the existence and autonomy of a world' (68, 83).

19. S. Kierkegaard writes: 'Only almighty power can withdraw itself by surrendering itself, and this relationship is the very independence of the recipient. God's almighty power is therefore his goodness. For goodness means surrendering oneself totally, but in such a way that by withdrawing oneself with almighty power one makes the recipient independent. All finite power creates dependence. Only almighty power can create independence – can bring forth out of nothing that which receives inward existence through the self-withdrawal of the almighty power' (quotation translated from the German *Gesammelte Werke,* Abteilung 17, Düsseldorf, 1954, 124).

20. M. Heidegger, *Being and Time,* trans. J. Macquarrie and E. Robinson, London, 1962, 63. See E. Jüngel's comment in 'The World as Possibility and Actuality. The ontology of the doctrine of justification' in *Theological Essays* I, trans. J. B. Webster, Edinburgh, 1989.

21. G. Picht, 'Die Zeit und die Modalitäten' in *Hier und Jetzt: Philosophieren nach Auschwitz und Hiroshima* I, Stuttgart, 1980, 362–74.

22. For more detail see J. Moltmann, 'Reflections on Chaos and God's Interaction with the world' in R. J. Russell (ed.), *Chaos and Complexity,* Notre Dame, 1995, 201–11.

V Eschatological Perspectives on the Future of the Universe

1. This is the expanded version of a lecture given at the Symposium of the John Templeton Foundation on 7–9 November 2000 in the Pontifical Academy of Science, Vatican City, Rome.

2. See J. Moltmann, *Experiences in Theology. Ways and Forms of Christian Theology,* trans. Margaret Kohl, London and Minneapolis, 2000, Part I, 6: Natural Theology, 64–83.

3. G. Liedke, *Im Bauch des Fisches. Ökologische Theologie,* Stuttgart, 1979; J. Moltmann, *God in Creation. An Ecological Doctrine of Creation* (the Gifford Lectures, 1984–85), trans. Margaret Kohl, London and San Francisco, 1985.

4. W. Pannenberg rightly uses for this the concept of *prolepsis,* anticipation; see his *Jesus, God and Man,* trans. L. C. Wilkins and D. A. Priebe, London and Philadelphia, 1968, 58ff.

5. S. Weinberg, *The First Three Minutes,* New York, 1988.

6. I am not using the term 'utopia' here in a negative sense, but positively, as it is used by Ernst Bloch in *The Principle of Hope,* trans. N. and S. Plaice and P. Knight, Cambridge, Mass., and Oxford, 1986.

7. For more detail, see J. Moltmann, *The Coming of God. Christian Eschatology,* trans. Margaret Kohl, London and Minneapolis, 1996.

7. See here E. Benz, *Schöpfungsglaube und Endzeiterwartung. Antwort auf Teilhard de Chardins Theologie der Evolution,* Munich, 1965; S. M. Daecke, *Teilhard de Chardin und die evangelische Theologie,* Göttingen, 1967.

9. This was shown by K. Löwith in *Meaning in History*, Chicago, 1949; see also the later expanded German version, *Weltgeschichte und Heilsgeschehen. Die theologischen Voraussetzungen der Geschichtsphilosophie*, Stuttgart, 1953.

10. J. Moltmann, *The Coming of God*, III, §8: End-Times of Human History: Exterminism, 202–18.

11. H. Schmid, *Die Dogmatik der Evangelisch-lutherischen Kirche, dargestellt und aus den Quellen belegt*, tenth ed., Gütersloh, 1983, 407. Also the comment by K. Stock, *Annihilatio Mundi. Johann Gerhards Eschatologie der Welt*, Munich, 1971.

12. The Doctrine Commission of the Church of England, *The Mystery of Salvation. The Story of God's Gift*, London, 1995, 199.

13. See here H. Küng, *Eternal Life?*, trans. E. Quinn, London, 1984.

14. H. Heppe and E. Bizer, *Die Dogmatik der Evangelisch-reformierten Kirche*, second ed., Neukirchen-Vluyn, 1958, 560.

15. D. Staniloae, *Orthodoxe Dogmatik*, Zürich and Gütersloh, 1985, 291: 'The world as the work of God's love, destined to be deified.'

16. C. Rowland, *The Open Heaven. A Study of Apocalyptic in Judaism and Early Christianity*, London, 1982.

17. J. Moltmann, *God in Creation*, VII: Heaven and Earth, 158–84.

18. F. W. J. Schelling, *Bruno, or On the Natural and Divine Principles of Things*, trans. M. Vater, Albany, NY, 1984.

19. K. Barth, *CD* III/2, 437f. See also my criticism in *The Coming of God*, 17–19.

20. See the time scheme of the physicist A. M. K. Müller, *Die präparierte Zeit*, Stuttgart, 1972, which I have pursued further in *God in Creation*, 129f., taking up M. Heidegger's saying: 'The primary phenomenon of primordial and authentic temporality is the future' (*Being and Time*, trans. J. Macquarrie and E. Robinson, London, 1962, 378).

21. On the term 'eschatological moment' and the relation to the 'primordial moment' see *The Coming of God*, 103–4 and 292–5.

22. F. Groth, *Die 'Wiederbringung aller Dinge' im württembergischen Pietismus*, Göttingen, 1984.

23. T. F. Torrance, *Divine and Contingent Order*, Oxford, 1981.

24. Thus S. Toulmin, *The Discovery of Time*, New York , 1965, 263: 'Are the laws of nature changing?', with reference to P. A. M. Dirac. Cf. also W. Pannenberg, *Erwägungen zu einer Theologie der Natur*, Göttingen, 1970, 65: 'Kontingenz und Naturgesetz.'

25. A. Koyré, *From the Closed World to the Infinite Universe*, Baltimore, 1957, 1968.

26. E. von Weizsäcker (ed.), *Offene Systeme 1: Beiträge zur Zeitstruktur von Information, Entropie und Evolution*, Stuttgart, 1974; K. Maurin, K. Michalski and E. Rudolph (eds), *Offene Systeme 2: Logik und Zeit*, Stuttgart, 1981.

VI What is Time and How Do We Experience It?

1. English-speaking readers familiar with Proust in C. K. Scott Moncrieff's great translation know the book as *Remembrance of Things Past*. But the original French title is *À la Recherche du Temps Perdu* – 'On the Search for Lost Time'.

2. I. Priogine and I. Stengers, *Time, Chaos and the New Laws of Nature* (trans. from French), London and New York, 1997.

3. C. F. von Weizsäcker, *Die Geschichte der Natur*, Göttingen, 1951.

4. I. Newton, *Philosophiae naturalis principia mathematica* [*Mathematical Principles of Natural Philosophy*], 1687, Scholium.

5. *Immanuel Kant's Critique of Pure Reason*, trans. N. Kemp Smith, revised ed., Edinburgh, 1933, 74f., 213f.

6. J. E. McTaggart, *The Nature of Existence*, Cambridge, 1927, §§305/5, differentiated these in A-series and B-series, but in the irreversible time we are discussing here, B is contained in A.

7. Aristotle, *Physics,* IV.13.

8. S. Kierkegaard, *The Concept of Dread*, trans. W. Lowrie, Princeton, 1944, 79. See here C. W. Thomsen and H. Holländer (eds), *Augenblick und Zeitpunkt*, Darmstadt, 1984.

9. E. Bloch, *Das Prinzip Hoffnung*, Frankfurt, 1959, 338 (*The Principle of Hope*, trans. N. and S. Plaice and P. Knight, Cambridge, Mass., and Oxford, 1986) ; E. Bloch, *Geist der Utopie*, revised ed., Berlin, 1923, 246 (no ET).

10. F. Cramer, *Der Zeitbaum. Grundlegung einer allgemeinen Zeittheorie*, Darmstadt, 1993, 40.

11. S. Kierkegaard, *The Concept of Dread,* 108.

12. E. Bloch, *Das Prinzip Hoffnung,* 224 (*The Principle of Hope*).

13. G. Picht, *Hier und Jetzt, Philosophie nach Auschwitz und Hiroshima* I, Stuttgart, 1980, 362ff.

14. S. Kierkegaard, *The Concept of Dread,* 80 (trans. slightly altered).

15. Augustine, *Confessions*, Book XI. 20, 26.

16. R. Koselleck, *Futures Past*, trans. K. Tribe, Cambridge, Mass., 1985.

17. 'Aeternitas . . . est interminibilis vitae tota . . . simul et perfecta possessio', Boethius, *The Consolation of Philosophy* V.6, trans. J. C. Relihan, Indianapolis, 2001.

18. For the discussion about this theology of time, cf. T. Freyer, 'Kontinuität und Unterbrechung. Theologische Anmerkungen zur Zeitproblematik bei J. Moltmann und J. B. Metz', *Theologie der Gegenwart* 38, 1995, 179–99.

VII *The Origin and Completion of Time in the Primordial and in the Eschatological Moment*

1. A. Schweitzer, *The Quest of the Hisorical Jesus,* trans. W. Montgomery, London, 1910 (= ET of first German edition [1906], which was published under the title *Vom Reimarus zu Wrede*), 396.

2. Cf. W. Schmidt, *Zeit und Ewigkeit. Die letzten Voraussetzungen der dialektischen Theologie,* Gütersloh, 1927; F. Holmström, *Das eschatologische Denken der Gegenwart,* Gütersloh, 1936.

3. P. Althaus, *Die Letzten Dinge. Entwurf einer christlichen Eschatologie,* Gütersloh, 1922, 84.

4. P. Althaus, *Die Letzten Dinge,* 98.

5. K. Barth, *Epistle to the Romans,* trans. from sixth ed. by E. C. Hoskyns, Oxford, 1933, 498 [trans. altered].

6. K. Barth, *Epistle to the Romans,* 497.

7. K. Barth, *The Resurrection of the Dead,* trans. H. J. Stenning, London, 1933, with the review by R. Bultmann in *Faith and Understanding* I, trans. Louise P. Smith, London, 1969. Both agreed in replacing the future which Paul expected in the form of an imminent cosmic event by the *futurum aeternum.*

8. F. D. E. Schleiermacher, *On Religion: Speeches to its Cultured Despisers,* trans. J. Oman, London, 1893, reissued New York, 1958, 101.

9.   Ich selbst bin Ewigkeit, wenn ich die Zeit verlasse
       und mich in Gott und Gott in mich zusammenfasse.

10. K. Barth, *Epistle to the Romans,* 195 [trans. altered]; see also his *Resurrection of the Dead.*

11. Cf. W. Pannenberg, 'Der Gott der Hoffnung' in S. Unseld (ed.), *Ernst Bloch zu ehren,* Frankfurt, 1965, 209–25, a contribution which I value particularly.

12. J. Moltmann, 'The Future as a New Paradigm of Transcendence' in *The Future of Creation,* trans. Margaret Kohl, London, 1979, 1–17.

13. J. Moltmann, *The Coming of God,* trans. Margaret Kohl, London and Minneapolis, 1996, 96–118.

14. M. Luther, WA 36, 349.

15. M. Luther, WA 14, 70.

16. Cf. G. Greshake and G. Lohfink, *Naherwartung – Auferstehung – Unsterblichkeit,* QD 71, fourth ed., Freiburg, 1982. This viewpoint is disputed in the Letter of the Congregation for the Doctrine of the Faith on Certain Questions of Eschatology (1979).

17. For the following passage I am indebted to E. A. Wyller's lecture 'Die Ewigkeitszeit Platons und die Endzeit der Johannes Apokalypse' in the FEST, Heidelberg 1986. Exegetically I am following W. Bousset, *Die Offenbarung Johannis,* Göttingen, 1906.

18. Words from the first verse of a hymn by Johann Rist (1607–67):

> O Ewigkeit, Zeit ohne Zeit . . .
> O Anfang sonder Ende.

19. See D. Staniloae, *Orthodoxe Dogmatik, Ökumenische Theologie*, vol. 12, Zürich and Gütersloh, 1985, 303–4.

20. The image is familiar to English-speaking readers from Isaac Watts's hymn:

> 'Time like an ever-rolling stream . . .'
> ('O God, our help in ages past')

VIII God and Space

1. See J. Moltmann, *God in Creation* (the Gifford Lectures 1984–85), trans. Margaret Kohl, London and San Francisco, 1985, Ch. VI.1: The Ecological Concept of Space, 142–5.

2. M. Heidegger, *Being and Time*, trans. J. Macquarrie and E. Robinson, London, 1962, §§22–4, 135–50, on the spatiality of Dasein; §28, 169–72, on Being-In as Such,. Cf. also O. F. Bollnow, *Mensch und Raum*, Stuttgart, 1963.

3. M. Jammer, *Concepts of Space*, Cambridge, Mass., 1954, Oxford, 1955, with a foreword by Albert Einstein.

4. Jammer, *Concepts of Space*, 28.

5. D. Staniloae, *Orthodoxe Dogmatik* I, Gütersloh and Einsiedeln, 1985, 189.

6. J. Moltmann, *The Trinity and the Kingdom of God*, trans. Margaret Kohl, London, 1981 [*The Trinity and the Kingdom*, San Francisco, 1981]; G. Greshake, *Der drei-eine Gott. Eine trinitarische Theologie*, Freiburg, 1997, M. Volf, *After our Likeness. The Church as the Image of the Trinity*, Grand Rapids, MI, 1998.

7. H. Denzinger, *Enchiridion Symbolorum*, twenty-third ed., Freiburg, 1947, 704; also *The Sources of Catholic Dogma*, trans. from the thirteenth ed. of Denzinger by R. J. Deferrari, St Louis and London, 1955. Cf. also P. Stemmer, 'Perichorese. Zur Geschichte eines Begriffs', *Archiv für Begriffsgeschichte* XXVII, 1983, 9–55.

8. Similarly Nouna Verna Harrison, 'Ein orthodoxer Zugang zum Geheimnis des dreieinigen Gottes. Fragen im Horizont des 21. Jahrhunderts', *Concilium* 37, 2001, 53.

9. J. Moltmann, *God in Creation*, 77ff.

10. M. Jammer, *Concepts of Space*, 46.

11. Nishida Kitaro, 'Was liegt dem Selbstsein zugrunde?' in *Logik des Ortes und die religiöse Weltanschauung*, trans. and ed. R. Elberfeld,

Darmstadt, 1999. Nishida founded the philosophical school of Kyoto (1870–1945).

12. J. Polkinghorne, 'Kenotic Creation and Divine Action' in J. Polkinghorne (ed.), *The Work of Love. Creation as Kenosis*, Grand Rapids, MI, 2001, 90–106, esp. 102–5.

13. P. Kuhn, *Gottes Selbsterniedrigung in der Theologie der Rabbinen*, Munich, 1968.

14. George Herbert (1593–1632), 'Christmas'. One of Luther's Christmas hymns traces the same idea of 'transcendence contracted to a span':

Den aller Welt Kreis nie umschloss / der liegt jetzt in Mariens Schoss,
Er ist ein Kindlein worden klein, / der alle Welt erhält allein
('Gelobet seisst du, Jesus Christ')

15. C. Link, *Schöpfung. Schöpfungstheologie angesichts der Herausforderungen des 20. Jahrhunderts*, Gütersloh, 1991, 582–600.

16. B. Pascal, *Pensées*, 206.

17. F. Nietzsche, *The Joyful Wisdom*, §125. Cf. *Complete Works*, trans. O. Levy, New York, 1974.

18. E. Loring, *I hear Hope Banging at my Back Door*, Atlanta, GA, 2000; S. T. Saunders and C. L. Campbell, *The Word on the Street. Performing Scriptures in the Urban Context*, Grand Rapids, MI., 2000, 143–75: Space.

IX *Humane Ethics and the Ethos of Biomedical Progress*

1. This question was asked several times at the CIBA Symposium in London in 1962. Cf. *Man and his Future*, a Ciba Foundation volume ed. G. E. W. Wolstenholme, London, 1963.

2. Julian Huxley, 'The Future of Man – evolutionary aspects' in *Man and his Future*, 3.

3. H. J. Müller, 'Genetic Progress by voluntarily conducted germinal choice' in *Man and his Future*.

4. Julian Huxley, 'The Future of Man' in *Man and his Future*, 6.

X *Science and Wisdom*

1. For more detail see J. Moltmann, *Experiences in Theology. Ways and Forms of Christian Theology*, trans. Margaret Kohl, London and Minneapolis, 2000, Part II, Ch. 4: Theological epistemology, 151–79.

2. In the present essay I am taking up the epilogue to the book cited in n. 1 above, and developing further what is said there on pages 334–43.

3. For more detail see J. Moltmann, *The Spirit of Life. A Universal Affirmation*, trans. Margaret Kohl, London and Minneapolis, 1992, Part I,

1 §2: Experience Subjectified and Methodologized in Modern Times: God in the Determining Subject, 28–31.

4. C. Böhme, *Für eine ökologische Naturästhetik,* Frankfurt, 1989.

5. See Ch. VI above: What is Time and How Do We Experience It?

6. I. Kant, Preface to the second ed. of the *Critique of Pure Reason,* trans. N. Kemp Smith, London, 1929, revised 1933, 20.

7. J. Polkinghorne, *Belief in God in an Age of Science,* New Haven and London, 1998, 1.

8. N. Maxwell, *From Knowledge to Wisdom: A Revolution in the Aims and Methods of Science,* Oxford, 1984; Mary Midgley, *Wisdom, Informations and Wonder. What is Knowledge for?,* London, 1989; Celia Deane-Drummond, *Creation through Wisdom,* Edinburgh, 2000. Of the literature published in German, I may mention G. Altner, G. Böhme and H. Ott (eds), *Naturerkennen und anerkennen. Über ethikrelevante Zugänge zur Natur,* Zug, Switzerland, 2000; M. Hailer, *Theologie als Weisheit. Sapientiale Konzeptionen in der Fundamentaltheologie des 20. Jahrhunderts,* Neukirchen, 1997; 'Figur und Thema der Weisheit in feministischen Theologien', *Internationale Theologie* VII, Frankfurt, 2001.

9. M. Pohlenz, *Die Stoa* II, Göttingen, 1949, 72.

10. G. von Rad, *Wisdom in Israel,* trans. J. D. Martin, London and Nashville, 1972. During the era of the Nazi dictatorship in Germany, with its blood-and-soil ideology, von Rad maintained the standpoint of revelation theology: God – human beings – nature. Israel first experienced the God of the Exodus in its history, in order then to go on to acknowledge him as the Creator of all things. In his book on Wisdom, written in old age, von Rad complemented his own theology of the Old Testament by the perspective God – nature – human beings. That is what is meant by his phrase 'the self-revelation of creation'.

11. This was especially pointed out by M. Welker in *Schöpfung und Wirklichkeit,* Neukirchen, 1995, 29 (ET *Creation and Reality,* trans. J. F. Hoffmeyer, Minneapolis, 1999).

12. It was this passage which led the Russian theologians and philosophers of religion V. Solovyov, P. Florensky, and especially S. Bulgakov to their strange – and in the Russian Orthodox Church disputed – sophiology. Cf. Celia Dean-Drummond's detailed account 'Sophia of the East' in her *Creation through Wisdom,* 75–111. On the distinction between the created, uncreated and – as I am proposing – the creative energies of God, see D. Reid, *Energies of the Spirit. Trinitarian Models in Eastern Orthodox and Western Theology,* Atlanta, 1997.

13. M. Pohlenz, *Die Stoa* II, 72.

14. G. Von Rad, *Wisdom in Israel.*

15. A. Pais, *Einstein lived here,* Oxford, 1994.

16. H. Müller, 'Zustand der atomaren Bedrohung', *EvTh* 60, 2000, 6, 479–80.

17. G. Altner, *Menschenwürde und biotechnischer Fortschritt im Horizont theologischer und sozialethischer Erwägungen,* special number *EvTh* 61, 2001. Cf. also G. Picht's older study, *Wahrheit, Vernunft, Verantwortung. Philosophische Studien,* Stuttgart, 1969, esp. 318–73: Der Begriff der Verantwortung. Struktur und Verantwortung der Wissenschaft im 20. Jahrhundert. Also H. Jonas, *Imperative of Responsibility,* trans. H. Jonas, Chicago, 1984.

XI 'From the Closed World to the Infinite Universe': The Case of Giordano Bruno

1. A. Koyré, *From the Closed World to the Infinite Universe,* Baltimore, 1968. Other literature: G. Bruno, *Opera latina conscripta,* ed. F. Fiorentino *et al.,* Naples and Florence, 1879–91, reprint 1962; *Von der Ursache, dem Prinzip und dem Einen* (German trans. of *De la causa, principio et uno*), PhB 21, fifth ed. 1977; *The Heroic Enthusiasts* (trans. by L. Williams of *Gli'heroici furori*), London, 1887; A. Croce, *Giordano Bruno. Der Ketzer von Nola,* Vienna, 1970; F. Stern, *Giordano Bruno – Vision einer Weltsicht,* Meisenheim, 1977; E. Grassi, *Zum Verständnis des Werkes: G. Bruno, Heroische Leidenschaften,* Hamburg, 1957; K, Huber, *Einheit und Vielheit in Denken und Sprache G. Brunos,* Winterthur, 1965; J. Brockmeier, *Die Naturtheorie Giordano Brunos,* Berlin, 1978; E. Jantsch, *The Self-Organizing Universe,* Oxford, 1980.

2. S. T. Coleridge, 'Frost at Midnight'.

3. In English translation:

> What God were this, who did but set the world in motion,
> who freely lets the universe its circles run?
> More proper far to move the world within,
> nature in him, himself in nature cherishing,
> so that what in him lives and moves and is,
> never his power, never his Spirit misses.

4. See S. T. Coleridge, *Biographica Literaria,* ed. J. Engell and W. Jackson Bate, Princeton, 1983, 145n.

XII TAO – The Chinese Mystery of the World: Lao Tsu's Tao Te Ching Read with Western Eyes

1. The translation in the present essay is by Gia-Fu Feng and Jane English, *Lao Tsu, Tao Te Ching,* Wildwood House, London, 1973. In some cases, however, it was necessary to modify this translation, in order to bring it into line with the translation used as basis for the German text. These modifications are enclosed in square brackets. Permission sought.

2. Instead of citing the extensive literature on Taoism with which I have concerned myself since my first visit to China in 1986, I should like to draw attention to the dissertation of my pupil Do Hoon Kim, *Der Taoismus und die christliche Schöpfungslehre. Ein Vergleich ihrer Grundideen aus ökologischer Sicht*, Tübingen, 1997.

3. See Dschuang Dsi, *Das wahre Buch vom südlichen Blütenland*, trans. R. Wilhelm, Munich, 1969, 88.

4. This has been very well worked out by G. Béky, *Die Welt des Tao*, Freiburg and Munich, 1972, Pt II: Das Tao und die phänomenale Welt, 99–146.

Previous Publication

I 'Theologie in der Welt der modernen Naturwissenschaften': Lecture on the occasion of the 31st Course for Further Medical Training in Regensburg on 10 October 1963, offprint Regensburg 1963; in *Perspectiven der Theologie*, Munich and Mainz, 1968, 269–87; in a translation by Margaret Clarkson in *Hope and Planning*, London and New York, 1971.

II 'Theologen und Naturwissenschaftler auf dem Weg zur Weisheit': Hitherto unpublished.

III 'Schöpfung als offenes System': Lecture to the Theological Society, Edinburgh, 9 April, 1975; in *Zukunft der Schöpfung*, Munich, 1977, 123–39, trans. as *The Future of Creation*, with 'Creation as an Open System' an earlier trans. of the present essay, also by Margaret Kohl, London and Philadelphia 1979, 115–30 (the German text of the essay has been slightly revised for the present publication).

IV 'Gottes Selbstbeschränkung und die Geschichte des Universums': Expanded text of a lecture to the conference of theologians and scientists sponsored by the John Templeton Foundation in Cambridge, October 1998; in J. Polkinghorne (ed.), *The Work of Love. Creation as Kenosis*, Grand Rapids and Cambridge, 2001.

V 'Eschatologische Perspektiven auf die Zukunft des Universums': Expanded text of a lecture for the conference of the John Templeton Foundation held in Vatican City, Rome, November 2000, on 'The Far-Future Universe: Eschatology from a Cosmic Perspective': hitherto unpublished.

VI 'Was ist Zeit und wie erfahren wir sie?': Lecture held in the university of Regensburg, 15 December 1998; in *Glauben und Denken*, 1, 1999, 139–54; in *Dialog. A Journal of Theology*, 39/1, 2000, 27–35.

VII 'Ursprung und Vollendung der Zeit im ursprunglichen und im eschatologischen Augenblick': In *Vernunft des Glaubens. Festschrift für Wolfhart Pannenberg zum 60. Geburtstag*, Göttingen, 1988, 578–92.

VIII 'Gott und Raum': Hitherto unpublished.

IX 'Humane Ethik und das Ethos des biomedizinischen Fortschritts': Revised text of a lecture held at the Hoffmann-La Roche Conference, Basle,

1971; earlier version in *Zukunft der Schöpfung,* 140–56, and the translation *The Future of Creation,* 131–48.

X 'Wissenschaft und Weisheit': Hitherto unpublished.

XI '"Was wär' ein Gott, der nur von aussen stiesse, das All der Welt am Finger laufen liesse . . ." Der Fall Giordano Bruno': In H. Häring und K. J. Kuschel (eds), *Gegenentwürfe. 24 Lebensläufe für eine andere Theologie. Festschrift für Hans Küng zum 60. Geburtstag,* Munich, 1988, 157–67.

XII 'TAO – das chinesische Geheimnis der Welt. Laotse's Tao-te-king mit westlichen Augen gelesen': In D. Becker (ed.), *Mit dem Fremden leben. Festschrift für Theo Sundermeier,* Erlangen, 2000, 123–38.

Index of Names